HEBREWS

WESLEY BIBLE STUDIES

Published by Wesleyan Publishing House
Indianapolis, Indiana 46250
Printed in the United States of America
ISBN: 978-0-89827-870-5
ISBN (e-book): 978-0-89827-871-2

CONTENTS

INTRODUCTION

Life Is Better Now

It wasn't long ago that computers, smartphones, iPads, air conditioning, and microwaves didn't exist. Life was low-tech or almost no-tech (from our perspective) in the old days. People often lined up at telephone booths to place a call, labored at manual typewriters, searched libraries for information, perspired at home and in their cars on hot days, and cooked meals the old-fashioned way—patiently on stovetop burners or in regular ovens. Today, however, we can establish communication immediately, get information instantly, enjoy cool comfort at home or as we drive, and prepare microwavable food within minutes or sometimes seconds. These are only a few of the ways life is better than it used to be.

Life is far better, too, for post-Calvary believers than it was for those who lived in Old Testament times. This is what the writer of Hebrews communicated in that lofty but practical book.

WE HAVE A BETTER PRIEST

The first section of Hebrews appealed to readers who were drifting away from the Christian faith because they preferred the visible forms and functions of Judaism. The writer of Hebrews urged them not to drift away, but by faith to perceive Jesus as better than the Old Testament prophets, the angels, and even Moses. Jesus, he explained, is God's risen Son, our Lord, and our High Priest. He provides eternal rest and intercedes for us at the Father's right hand. Through Him, we can approach the throne of grace at any time and lay any request or burden there.

WE HAVE A BETTER SACRIFICE

In Old Testament times, priests offered multiple sacrifices for sin; and annually, on the Day of Atonement, Israel's high priest carried the blood of a bull and a goat into the Most Holy Place for a covering for his sins and for the people's sins. But by offering His own blood on the cross as a once-for-all, perfect sacrifice, Jesus, our High Priest, removed our sins forever. Hebrews 10:11–12 declares: "Day after day every priest stands and performs his religious duties; again and again he offers the same sacrifices, which can never take away sins. But when this priest [Jesus] had offered for all time one sacrifice for sins, he sat down at the right hand of God."

WE HAVE A BETTER COVENANT

The old covenant that God delivered through Moses to the Israelites in the wilderness showed them God is holy and requires holiness of His people, but it could never make them holy. The covenant of law revealed sin but was powerless to remove it. Its purpose was to show the people how desperately they needed the Redeemer, the Messiah. By contrast, Christ is the mediator of a new covenant (Heb. 9:15), and all who have believed in Him have the new covenant written on their hearts.

As we study Hebrews, we will marvel at the privileges we enjoy as God's redeemed children. Life is better for us than it was for those who lived under the old covenant, but with privilege comes responsibility. As God's responsible children, let us pursue holiness, engage in fervent prayer, live by faith, love our heavenly Father and one another, cling to the promises, and loyally follow Jesus all the way home!

1

THE FINALITY OF GOD'S SALVATION

Hebrews 1:1–14

Jesus alone is the source of redeeming grace.

A list of the world's most admired people might include powerful political leaders, record-holding athletes, outstanding musicians, philanthropists, gifted authors, successful educators, well-known scientists, and dedicated preachers. But not even the most admired person deserves the kind of esteem that we should ascribe to Jesus. As the writer to the Hebrews pointed out, He is even higher than the angels, because He is God's glorious Son. He embodies God's message, sustains the universe, and owns the right to receive worship and to reign forever.

This study will inspire you to bow humbly before Jesus and to serve Him lovingly and faithfully. You will see that no human being, regardless of his or her credentials or accomplishments, can compare with Jesus.

COMMENTARY

Perhaps no letter in the New Testament is more mysterious to modern Christian audiences than the epistle to the Hebrews. There are a few reasons for this: (1) We can't say with any certainty who the author was; (2) we can't say with any certainty who the original recipients of the letter were; and (3) we find it hard to account for the unusual emphasis on seemingly esoteric subjects like the angels, the Old Testament sacrificial system, and the obscure priest Melchizedek. More than any other New Testament

book (with the possible exception of Revelation), the epistle to the Hebrews feels like it's coming to us from another world.

Yet, there is much we can say with confidence about this letter and much to be gained by a careful reading of it. The author was almost certainly a converted Christian Jew, and he had a passionate and pastoral heart for the people to whom the letter was addressed. The intended recipients of the letter were also Jewish Christians. They had already experienced persecution as a result of their faith in Jesus (Heb. 10:32–34), and it seems that they were trying to strengthen their resolve for an expected second round of persecution, this time more severe (12:3–4). Some of them, however, were probably tempted by the thought of returning to their Judaism (10:35–36), since it was a protected religion in the Empire. This letter, written in the form of a sermon, was intended to strengthen their faith and steel their resolve to follow Jesus whatever may come.

Jesus, the Image of God (Heb. 1:1–7)

The theme of Hebrews might best be summarized by a single verse near the end of the letter: "Let us fix our eyes on Jesus, the author and perfecter of our faith, who for the joy set before him endured the cross, scorning its shame, and sat down at the right hand of the throne of God" (12:2). It is clear that the author had his eyes fixed on Jesus from the first sentence: **In the past God spoke to our forefathers through the prophets at many times and in various ways, but in these last days he has spoken to us by his Son, whom he appointed heir of all things, and through whom he made the universe** (1:1–2).

With that power-packed opening sentence, the author focused his readers' eyes on Jesus and established a theme and pattern that would carry through the entire letter: The Old Testament, or old covenant, was great, but it was always intended to point the way forward to something better. **God spoke to our forefathers**

through the prophets (v. 1), who would have included not only the "writing prophets" like Isaiah and Jeremiah, but also men and women like Moses, Deborah, Samuel, and David. Such were the heroes of the Jewish faith, and the author of Hebrews did not diminish their importance. Yet, one had come who was greater than all the prophets who had gone before: **his Son** (v. 2).

WORDS FROM WESLEY

Hebrews 1:1

God, who at sundry times—The creation was revealed in the time of Adam, the last judgment in the time of Enoch; and so at various times and in various degrees more explicit knowledge was given, *in divers manners*—In visions, in dreams, and by revelations of various kinds. Both these are opposed to the one entire and perfect revelation which He has made to us by Jesus Christ. The very number of the prophets showed, that they prophesied only *in part; of old*—There were no prophets for a large tract of time before Christ came, that the great prophet might be the more earnestly expected: *spake*—A part is put for the whole, implying every kind of divine communication, *by the prophets*—The mention of whom is a virtual declaration, that the apostle received the whole Old Testament, and was not about to advance any doctrine in contradiction to it: *hath in these last times*—Intimating that no other revelation is to be expected: *spoken*—All things, and in the most perfect manner, *by his Son*—Alone (ENNT)

In a flurry of phrases designed to put the superiority of Jesus beyond dispute, the author of Hebrews forcefully demonstrated how Jesus surpassed the greatest of the great men and women of the faith. In the process, the author introduced many of the themes to which he would later return. Jesus was **appointed heir of all things** and it was through Him God **made the universe**. He was **the radiance of God's glory and the exact representation of his being**. He **provided purification for sins** and then **sat down at the right hand of the Majesty in heaven** (vv. 2–3). While the Old Testament prophets, from Moses to Malachi, had given a true and accurate representation of God's Word, Jesus *became* God's Word to His creation, in three dimensions and high-definition.

Many students of Scripture have puzzled over why the author of Hebrews felt it necessary to assert Jesus' superiority over the angels. There was a well-established Jewish tradition that taught that God had delivered His law to Moses by angels. In a sense, then, the angels seemed to hold an even higher place as messengers of God than the great prophets did. So the author wanted there to be no mistake; not only was Jesus superior to the prophets, but He was **superior to the angels** as well (v. 4). Jesus had a special relationship with God as His **Father** that the angels were not privileged to enjoy. He was God's **Son**, the Messiah, Israel's true king (vv. 5–6; quoting from Ps. 2:7 and 2 Sam. 7:14). The angels, on the other hand, were instructed to **worship him** (Heb. 1:6; perhaps quoting Ps. 97:7), because they were **his servants** (Heb. 1:7; quoting Ps. 104:4); only Jesus was **the exact representation of his being** (Heb. 1:3).

WORDS FROM WESLEY

Hebrews 1:5

Thou art my Son—God of God, light of light; *this day have I begotten thee*—I have begotten thee from eternity, which, by its unalterable permanency of duration, is one continued unsuccessive day. *I will be to him a Father, and he shall be to me a son*—I will own myself to be His Father, and Him to be my Son, by eminent tokens of my peculiar love. The former clause relates to His natural sonship, by an eternal, inconceivable generation, the other to His Father's acknowledgment and treatment of Him, as His incarnate Son. Indeed this promise related immediately to Solomon, but in a far higher sense to the Messiah. (ENNT)

Jesus, the Just Judge (Heb. 1:8–9)

After a one-verse description of the angels' role as servants (v. 7), the author spent the rest of this first chapter focusing on the contrasting role of Jesus as Lord. First, he quoted Psalm 45:6–7, which described the coming Messiah as a just judge. The psalm as a whole was a wedding song written about the king of Israel (45:1); it described him (and his bride) in glowing, almost godlike terms. In fact, the most straightforward translation of verse 6 reads as if the psalmist was addressing the king as "God." Uncomfortable with this, many have tried to find an alternate translation or interpretation. But the author of Hebrews had no trouble with it; he interpreted it as referring to Jesus.

Earlier, the author said that Jesus, after dealing with our sins, "sat down at the right hand of the Majesty in heaven" (Heb. 1:3). This is a way of saying that Jesus had assumed the position of power and authority over the universe. The verses quoted here, from Psalm 45, returned to this theme, equating the godlike king of the Psalm with Jesus: **Your throne, O God, will last for ever and ever** (Heb. 1:8). When Jesus returned to heaven, God made Him king; and the throne will belong to Him for eternity. While the angels are merely servants, Jesus has the power and authority to administer the kingdom forever.

Throughout the Old Testament, the kings of Israel and other nations were judged according to their desire and capacity to administer justice and righteousness within their kingdoms. Too often, even the kings of Judah and Israel allowed injustice and wickedness to go unchecked on their watch. By contrast, Jesus' reign will be characterized by justice: **and righteousness will be the scepter of** His **kingdom** (v. 8). While we tend to think of justice in terms of someone getting the punishment he or she deserves, the biblical concept of justice is broader than that. It includes the idea of making right what was wrong. Part of God's vision for His kingdom is that there will no longer be a place for sin or wickedness.

According to the psalm, this was Jesus' primary qualification for becoming king: **You have loved righteousness and hated wickedness; therefore God, your God, has set you above your companions by anointing you with the oil of joy** (v. 9). While, at one level, we can say, "Of course, Jesus would be king. He's God's Son," at another level, we should remember that He earned the role of king by demonstrating a passion for justice and righteousness by His journey to the cross.

Jesus, Creator and Re-Creator (Heb. 1:10–12)

Jesus' superiority over the angels is also demonstrated by His role in creation. We have already seen a quick hit on this theme in verse 2, where the author of Hebrews said that Jesus was superior to the prophets because He is God's "Son . . . through whom he made the universe." Here, the author returned to that theme in relation to the angels, quoting from Psalm 102: **In the beginning, O Lord, you laid the foundations of the earth, and the heavens are the work of your hands** (Heb. 1:10). There is nothing to suggest that these verses in Psalm 102 were ever understood to be a reference to the Messiah, so it is somewhat surprising that the author of Hebrews applied them to Jesus at this point. However, since he had already taken the step of equating Jesus with God, it was not a stretch to say Jesus performed this act that had always been attributed to God.

A significant part of the Jewish hope was the belief that one day God, through the Messiah, would create new heavens and a new earth, where justice, righteousness, and peace would endure forever (see, for example, Isa. 65:17–25). Just as Jesus was presumably involved in the creation of the heavens and earth, the author of Hebrews suggested that He would be the one to oversee the transition to the new heavens and earth: **They will perish, but you remain; they will all wear out like a garment. You will roll them up like a robe; like a garment they will be**

changed. But you remain the same, and your years will never end (Heb. 1:11–12). The angels will also make the transition to the next age, just as all the saints in Christ will; but it will not be the saints, prophets, or angels who will remove the "robe" of the current universe and roll it up; none of them will give the heavens and earth a new change of clothes. That task is reserved for the Lord, the king, Jesus. Just as He created the heavens and earth that have been our home in the past and present, He will create the new heavens and earth that will serve as our eternal home.

WORDS FROM WESLEY

Hebrews 10:10–12

He is a wise man, even in God's account; for "he buildeth his house upon a rock;" upon the Rock of Ages, the everlasting Rock, the Lord Jesus Christ. Fitly is He so called; for He changeth not: He is "the same yesterday, and today, and for ever." To Him both the man of God of old, and the apostle citing his words, bear witness: "Thou, Lord, in the beginning hast laid the foundation of the earth; and the heavens are the works of thine hands: They shall perish; but thou remainest: And they all shall wax old as doth a garment; and as a vesture shalt thou fold them up, and they shall be changed: But thou art the same, and thy years shall not fail" (Heb. 1:10–12). Wise, therefore, is the man who buildeth on Him; who layeth Him for his only foundation; who builds only upon His blood and righteousness, upon what He hath done and suffered for us. On this corner-stone he fixes his faith, and rests the whole weight of his soul upon it. (WJW, vol. 5, 428)

Jesus, the True King (Heb. 1:13–14)

Finally, the author of Hebrews described the role of the Messiah, Jesus, as the true king. This quote comes from Psalm 110: **Sit at my right hand until I make your enemies a footstool for your feet** (Heb. 1:13). The quotation is the first verse of the most quoted psalm in the New Testament. Peter, Paul, the author of Hebrews, and even Jesus himself (according to Matthew, Mark, and Luke) referred to this psalm in their efforts to interpret and explain what it means that Jesus is Messiah. In fact, the author of Hebrews would come back to it again later. The psalm described the enthronement of the Messiah as king at God's right hand and the inevitable defeat of every enemy of God. Again, the writer of Hebrews argued that such an honor was never given to an angel. They are ministers; not kings. They don't administer justice, righteousness, redemption, or salvation; their role is to **serve those who will inherit salvation** (v. 14). The fact that Jesus is the Messiah, the eternal king seated at God's right hand, demonstrates His superiority over the prophets and angels.

While it is difficult for modern readers to jump into the first chapter of Hebrews and grasp the flow of its argument, the original recipients of the letter would have had no problem getting the point. Some of them were considering returning to their original Judaism; all of them would be faced with the choice of being faithful to Christ or being obedient to Caesar. But the author of Hebrews, the passionate pastor, argued that now that the people knew Jesus, there could be no turning back to the prophets who spoke God's word or the angels who (according to tradition) delivered God's law. Both the prophets and angels were simply messengers who pointed forward to Jesus—the one true Lord, Redeemer, and King.

DISCUSSION

Many people, even those who are not Christian, hold Jesus in high regard, but the author of Hebrews describes Jesus as someone who is uniquely worthy of our adoration and worship.

1. How would you use Hebrews 1:1–2 to refute the claim that God has never been involved in history?

2. What works and ministries does the writer to the Hebrews ascribe to Jesus in verses 2–3?

3. If a cultist told you Jesus was a high-ranking angel, how would you answer him or her (vv. 4–9)?

4. What significance do you find in the fact that Jesus sat down at God's right hand "after he had provided purification for sins" (v. 3)?

5. How does the fact that Jesus occupies an everlasting throne (v. 8) help you face troubled times?

6. What evidence of Jesus' almighty power do you find in verses 10–13?

7. How will your worship of Jesus be more meaningful because of the portrayal of Him in Hebrews 1:1–14?

8. How does this passage motivate you to tell others about Jesus?

PRAYER

Heavenly Father, thank You for giving us Your Son, who is the exact representation of Your being. To see Jesus is to see You.

2

TREASURE YOUR GREATEST TREASURE

Hebrews 2:1–18

Stay firmly anchored to the truth revealed in Jesus Christ.

Two boaters in their mid-twenties will never forget June 2, 2011. That was the day their craft lost power on the river above Niagara Falls and drifted within seven hundred feet of Horseshoe Falls on the Canadian side of the river. Using a cell phone, they issued an urgent plea for help and received it in the nick of time. The Erie County Sheriff's Marine Unit arrived within minutes and used a rope to tow the boaters to safety.

Drifting toward Niagara Falls is certainly perilous, but drifting away from biblical truth is even more so because it endangers the soul. This study offers strong incentives to stay firmly anchored to the truth and committed to Jesus Christ.

COMMENTARY

For at least five hundred years, the Christian church has been embroiled in a debate over the theological doctrines of perseverance and apostasy. The question has been debated endlessly—especially between Calvinists and Arminians—whether a person who is a true believer can later reject the faith. Those who argue for perseverance say that a true believer will persevere to the end and be saved; God guarantees it, they say. Those who argue for the possibility of apostasy say that a person's genuine faith today offers no guarantee that he or she will continue in faith to the end, because faith is a matter of the human will. Those who argue for perseverance say that a person who commits apostasy (abandons their faith) was never a genuine Christian at any time. The person who argues for the possibility of apostasy says that while God is always faithful, humans sometimes break faith.

The debate over the theology of perseverance and apostasy often mires down in technical, theoretical, and philosophical wrangling. When the arguments turn to Scripture, however, much of the biblical focus in this theological debate rests on the letter to the Hebrews. The Hebrew Christians, who had already experienced one round of persecution were facing the possibility of another round. Many were afraid and tempted to abandon their Christian faith and return to the safer confines of Judaism. In response, the author of Hebrews included several strongly worded warnings in his letter to them. The first of these is in the first part of today's passage (2:1–4). For the author and his readers, however, this was no theological debate. They were not attempting to discover a definitive answer to a theoretical, philosophical question. They were in the midst of real life, facing genuine danger, and they needed practical guidance and wisdom. Thus, the author of Hebrews warned them, in no certain terms, to cling to and avoid falling away from their faith in Jesus Christ.

Jesus—Don't Neglect Him (Heb. 2:1–4)

After a majestic first chapter, in which the author of Hebrews helped his readers focus their eyes on Jesus, the one who is superior to the Old Testament prophets and the angels who (in Jewish tradition) delivered the law to Moses, he paused his argumentation long enough to make a direct application of this truth to his readers: **We must pay more careful attention** (v. 1). It is interesting that the author did not simply tell his readers to "stay the course" or to keep doing what they were doing in spite of the threat of persecution. Instead, he essentially said, "If you're tempted to turn back, you need to go deeper. There's more to Jesus than you know." The danger the author had in mind was clear; he was concerned that they would **drift away** (v. 1) from their faith in Jesus. When you're in a boat, drifting is not usually the result of a conscious decision but because of distraction. So in faith, people do not usually intend to drift away. Instead, they become distracted, lose their focus, and even stop caring, until they suddenly find themselves in waters that are too dangerous for them to handle. So the author urged his readers to **pay more careful attention . . . to what** they had **heard** (v. 1).

The readers of this letter were distracted by the threat of persecution and in danger of losing their focus on and interest in Jesus. They were attracted to the relative safety and comfort they felt under the Jewish Law. So the author of Hebrews reminded his readers about the importance with which God treated the law: **the message spoken by angels was binding, and every violation and disobedience received its just punishment** (v. 2). If God's administration of the old covenant delivered by the angels was so strict and severe, He would certainly not be lax in administering the new covenant delivered by His own Son. **How shall we escape if ignore such a great salvation** (v. 3)? The old and new covenants are the same in the sense that there are covenant stipulations or requirements and then blessings that come to those who keep the covenants and curses on those who break them. God had proven himself faithful in keeping the old covenant, both in the blessings and curses. We should not think that He will be any looser in administering the blessings and curses of the new covenant.

Then the author reminded his readers of what they already knew about this new covenant but to which they needed to pay more careful attention. **This salvation . . . was first announced by the Lord** (v. 3). This time God did not send His message via His messengers, the angels. This time the King showed up to deliver the message in person. What do you expect would happen if you ignored or neglected a message that was so important the

King delivered it in person? **This salvation** also **was confirmed to us by those who heard him** (v. 3). This phrase strongly suggests that the author of Hebrews was not an original disciple or the apostle Paul, one of those who had personally received the message of salvation from Jesus. The message was confirmed by eyewitnesses who faithfully passed it on to the author of Hebrews and his readers. Even more than that, **God also testified to it by signs, wonders and various miracles, and gifts of the Holy Spirit distributed according to his will** (v. 4). The Spirit testifies directly to our hearts the truth of the message of salvation, as we find that God is transforming our hearts, giving us the ability to become the people He has called us to be.

WORDS FROM WESLEY

Hebrews 2:3

So great a salvation—A deliverance from so great wickedness and misery, into so great holiness and happiness. This was first *spoken of* (before he came it was not known) *by* Him who is *the Lord*—Of angels as well as men; *and was confirmed to us*—Of this age, even every article of it; *by them that had heard him*—And had been themselves also both eyewitnesses and ministers of the word. (ENNT)

Jesus, the True Man (Heb. 2:5–9)

After his stern warning about paying more careful attention to what they had heard about Jesus, the author of Hebrews returned to the argument he had put forth in the first chapter, picking up some of its threads and expanding on them. In chapter 1, he had spoken about the superiority of Jesus over the angels (vv. 4–7, 14) and about the transition from creation to new creation, from the present age to the age to come (vv. 10–12). Here, he returned to both themes as he reflected on the authority structure of the new world: **It is not to angels that he has subjected the world to come, about which we are speaking** (2:5). The angels will presumably survive the transition, but they will still have a subordinate role in the new heavens and earth.

WORDS FROM WESLEY

Hebrews 2:6

What is man—To the vast expanse of heaven, to the moon and the stars which thou hast ordained? This Psalm seems to have been composed by David, in a clear moon-shiny and star-light night, while he was contemplating the wonderful fabric of heaven: because in his magnificent description of its luminaries, he takes no notice of the sun, the most glorious of them all. The words here cited concerning dominion, were doubtless, in some sense, applicable to Adam; although in their complete and highest sense, they belong to none but the second Adam: *or the son of man, that thou visitest him*—The sense rises, we are mindful of Him that is absent; but to visit denotes the care of a present God. (ENNT)

The quotation in verses 6–7 is from Psalm 8:4–6. The word translated **man** is the Hebrew word for *human*. The phrase **son of man** is a Hebrew idiom that meant something like "average Joe." However, the prophet Daniel invested this common Hebrew idiom with a deeper level of meaning, when he used the phrase to refer to the coming Messiah: "In my vision at night I looked, and there before me was one like a son of man, coming with the clouds of heaven. He approached the Ancient of Days and was led into his presence. He was given authority, glory and sovereign power; all peoples, nations and men of every language worshiped him. His dominion is an everlasting dominion that will not pass away, and his kingdom is one that will never be destroyed" (Dan. 7:13–14). Jesus often referred to himself as the "Son of Man" in this Daniel 7 sense. Psalm 8 teaches that God's plan was to give humanity His glory and the authority to rule over His creation; however, humanity fell short of the calling to reflect God's glory. Daniel 7 prophesied that there would be another human who would not fail in this vocation. The author of Hebrews said that man was Jesus: **In putting everything under him, God left nothing that is not subject to him** (Heb. 2:8).

The only problem, according to the author of Hebrews, is that **at present we do not see everything subject to him** (v. 8). And we may echo a hearty "amen." As we look at the world around us, we see so much poverty, injustice, and unrighteousness. In some ways, it appears that humanity is doing no better at administering God's creation than we ever have since the beginning of time. The difference is, however, **we see Jesus**. We see the true and faithful human being. He was **made** like us, **a little lower than the angels. . . . He suffered death** like all humanity has or will. But He is **now crowned with glory and honor** (v. 9). He has pioneered the way for us, demonstrating what it means to reflect God's glory and effectively administer His creation. In suffering a sacrificial death, He became our representative—standing in our place, doing what we could never do—so that we can be transformed and take our place alongside Him as part of the new, redeemed humanity.

Jesus, the Older Brother (Heb. 2:10–18)

Jesus once (or perhaps many times) told a parable about a young man who cashed in his inheritance, wasted it on hedonistic pleasures, and then returned home to an unexpected welcome by his father. Perhaps the greatest villain of the story is the older brother, who was jealous and refused to welcome the younger brother home. As the author of Hebrews continued to focus his readers' eyes on Jesus, he presented Him as the older brother; but he is not *that* kind of older brother. Instead, Jesus is the older brother that provides true leadership and takes genuine responsibility for His siblings: **Both the one who makes men holy and those who are made holy are of the same family. So Jesus is not ashamed to call them brothers** (v. 11).

It was hinted in the previous section about how part of Jesus' vocation was in **bringing many sons to glory** (v. 10) to help us find our way again to the place where we are reflecting God's glory. The pathway the older brother had to take to make this happen was one of suffering: **it was fitting that God . . . should make the author of their salvation perfect through suffering** (v. 10). The quotation in verse 12 might not be familiar, but the passage from which it comes is well-known. Psalm 22 is the classic prophecy of Jesus' crucifixion, and the verse quoted begins the conclusion of the psalmist's account of the Messiah's suffering. The two quotations in Hebrews 2:13—from Isaiah 8:17 and 18—emphasizes that Jesus claims us as part of His family. He is the kind of older brother who will suffer the worst so that we can have the opportunity for the best. Again, we might ask, "How shall we escape if we ignore such a great salvation?" (Heb. 2:3).

WORDS FROM WESLEY

Hebrews 2:12

I will declare thy name to my brethren—Christ declares the name of God, gracious and merciful, plenteous in goodness and truth, to all who believe, that they also may praise Him: *In the midst of the church will I sing praise unto thee*—As the precentor of the choir. This He did literally, in the midst of His apostles, on the night before His passion. And as it means, in a more general sense, setting forth the praise of God, He has done it in the church by His word and His Spirit; He still does, and will do it, throughout all generations. (ENNT)

Jesus was the true man—the older brother of the new, transformed humanity—and because He was willing to suffer on our behalf, He is bringing many to glory. This points to another reason for the superiority of Jesus: through His sacrificial death, He became the true high priest and destroyed forever the power of sin and death. He could not do this without taking His place among His younger brothers and sisters. He could not remain aloof. **Since the children have flesh and blood, he too shared in their humanity so that by his death he might destroy him who holds the power of death. . . . For this reason he had to be made like his brothers in every way** (vv. 14, 17). It is only because Jesus was willing to be made "a little lower than the angels" (v. 7) and be made **perfect through suffering** (v. 10) that He could **become a merciful and faithful high priest in service to God** (v. 17). For all of these reasons, Jesus is perfectly suited **to help those who are being tempted** (v. 18), which is exactly the situation in which the Hebrew Christians were finding themselves. Thus, the author's exhortation to "pay more careful attention . . . to what we have heard, so that we do not drift away" (v. 1).

WORDS FROM WESLEY

Hebrews 3:17

Wherefore it behooved him—It was highly fit and proper, yea, necessary, in order to His design of redeeming them; *to be made in all things*—That essentially pertain to human nature, and in all sufferings and temptations; *like his brethren*—This is a recapitulation of all that goes before; the sum of all that follows is added immediately; *that he might be a merciful and faithful high-priest*—Merciful towards sinners; faithful towards God. A priest or high-priest is one who has a right of approaching God, and of bringing others to Him. Faithful is treated of, ch. 3:2, &c. with its use. Merciful, ch. 4:14, &c. with the use also. High-priest, ch. 5:4, &c. ch. 7:1, &c. The use is added from ch. 10:19 in things pertaining to God, *to expiate the sins of the people*—Offering up their sacrifices and prayers to God, deriving God's grace, peace, and blessings, upon them. (ENNT)

DISCUSSION

Theologians have debated the possibility of apostasy for centuries, but the author of Hebrews treats it as a genuine danger, warning hearers to hold on to their faith.

1. What do you think the writer was referring to by "what we have heard" (Heb. 2:1)?
2. What do you think causes someone to drift away?
3. Why do you agree or disagree that even a "seasoned" believer may drift away?
4. Why do you agree or disagree that a believer may ignore salvation?
5. According to verse 4, what was the purpose of apostolic "signs, wonders and various miracles"?
6. According to verses 9–15, what did Jesus accomplish by His death?
7. How has Jesus, your "merciful and faithful high priest" (v. 17), helped you in the past week?
8. Why is Jesus able to help you when you are tempted (v. 18)?
9. How has a truth in Hebrews 2:1–18 anchored your faith more firmly?

PRAYER

Lord, help us to pay close attention to our faith and to take nothing You have given us for granted. Help us endure and overcome temptation like Jesus did.

3

FIX YOUR EYES ON JESUS

Hebrews 3:1–19

Keep your focus on Jesus so that sin will not draw you away.

A physical examination is incomplete if it does not include the heart. A healthy heart pumps blood effectively to every part of the body and helps us lead a strong, energetic, and vigorous life. Physicians and nutritionists encourage us to eat properly and exercise regularly. However, temptations to neglect the heart assail us. Junk food is readily available, and the couch or recliner may seem more inviting than a treadmill or an elliptical. Nevertheless, junk food and a sedentary lifestyle can clog our arteries and contribute to heart disease.

This study emphasizes the need to guard our hearts from unbelief and sin's deceitfulness and thereby avoid hardening of the "hearteries."

COMMENTARY

The letter to the Hebrews is what we would call a systematic theology. That is, it begins with a basic premise—that Jesus is "the radiance of God's glory and the exact representation of his being" (1:3). The rest of the work is a system of "therefores," building a logical framework of beliefs and ethics based on the basic premise. Therefore, we must study Hebrews from the beginning and keep in mind everything we learn as we go along.

Another premise of the letter is the validity of the old covenant as revealed by God in the Old Testament. The author repeatedly acknowledged the worth and usefulness of the old covenant. However, he made the case that Jesus fulfilled the old covenant and introduced a new covenant. The author challenged his readers to wrestle with the concept of a *new* covenant. There is something qualitatively different about the covenant we have in Christ as compared to the covenant the Hebrews had in Moses and the prophets. The new covenant is not the old covenant only better. It is a new way of understanding the relationship between God and His creation; it includes old covenant concepts and introduces new revelation that the old covenant was unable to sustain.

Throughout the letter, the author warned the Hebrews not to fall into the temptation of relying on the old covenant. This would have been easy because that is what they knew and what was familiar. The old covenant was restrictive and prescriptive. The new covenant is universal and descriptive. The analogy the author used is that of food. When we are young, we live on milk because we have no choice. Our bodies cannot digest solid foods. As we grow, we eat solid foods, and we choose those foods that we will eat. It is a move from sustenance to nutrition, from survival to living.

The author was careful to make clear that he was writing for "we who have believed" (4:3). His immediate audience was Jews who believed Jesus is the Christ. He relied heavily on their knowledge of Scripture and tradition. His concern was that believers did not come to depend on their faith as a system of religion which contains a formula for faith, but that "faith is being sure of what we hope for and certain of what we do not see" (11:1).

Modern Christians need to study Hebrews in a similar fashion. After we have been in the church for awhile, we are tempted to rely on our goodness and good deeds as merits for our salvation. We can come to believe the way we worship is the best way, the way we run our church is the way everyone should run their church. The passage we are studying today is exactly on that point. We must be diligent to remain in a constant state of faith so the things we see around us do not become more important to us than Jesus, whom we cannot see.

Jesus Is the Center of Our Faith (Heb. 3:1–6)

Verse 1 of chapter 3 is a summary of everything written in the first two chapters. It is a transition statement from the detailed description of Jesus (ch. 1) and the relationship between Jesus, God, and humanity (ch. 2) into a description of the implications of our faithfulness (ch. 3). The letter focuses our thoughts on relationships, and this passage emphasizes the relationship between believers and Jesus and between believers and sin.

Verse 1 shows us the importance of understanding these relationships in this order. Jesus is described as **the apostle and high priest whom we confess**. The **apostle** was the one sent with the good news of salvation. The **high priest** was the one who made atonement for the sin of the people. Our relationship with Jesus is the basis for dealing with sin. If the former relationship is not right, then the latter relationship is hopeless. Our relationship with Jesus is based on Him, not us.

Dietrich Bonhoeffer said that anyone who would take up Christianity must discard as irrelevant two questions: "How am I to be good?" and "How am I to do good?" Instead, he said, the Christian must ask the utterly different question, "What is the will of God?" Hebrews tells us that to know Jesus is to know the will of God. God's will is not ethereal, but personal and tangible as incarnated in Christ. We can only understand ourselves as the center of God's affection if we make Jesus the center of our affection, as a person, not a concept or religious structure.

Verses 2–5 acknowledge the benefits of religious concepts and structure. Many people object to what they call "institutionalized religion," but institutionalization is as necessary to human function as shelter is necessary for human survival. We need organization. We need set boundaries so we can determine right and wrong beliefs, right and wrong actions. However, we must always remember that houses are made for people to live in, and organizations are made to help people grow. The author wrote, **the builder of a house has greater honor than the house itself** (v. 3). He encouraged us to remember that the church is for the people. If the church becomes more important than the people, we have slipped into idolatry and the new covenant is of no use to us.

WORDS FROM WESLEY

Hebrews 3:3

The heavenly calling—God calls from heaven, and to heaven, by the gospel: *consider the apostle*—The messenger of God, who pleads the cause of God with us: *and high-priest*—Who pleads our cause with God. Both are contained in the one word Mediator. He compares Christ as an apostle with Moses; as a priest with Aaron. Both these offices, which Moses and Aaron severally bore, he bears together, and far more eminently: *of our profession*—The religion we profess. (ENNT)

The author emphasized this point in verse 6 when he wrote that **we are his house, if we hold on to our courage and the hope of which we boast.** So what is this courage and hope? We must fix our thoughts on Jesus to know. He hung on the cross and said, “Father, forgive them, for they do not know what they are doing” (Luke 23:34). He said to pray for our enemies and bless those who persecute us. He said to give forgiveness every time it is requested. He showed us that relationships—people—are worth dying for. If we try to save our lives, we will lose them. If we lose them for His sake, we will find eternal life.

Christianity Is a Relationship with God (Heb. 3:7–11)

Because Christianity is based on relationships, it is a way of living, a way of being marked by revelation and action. Sometimes we focus so much on our sin and our need of a Savior that we treat our faith as only an end to sinning rather than the beginning of an intimate relationship with a holy God, one that will result in holy behavior. This allows us to objectify our faith and neglect the God of our faith. That is, we develop mental checklists to judge ourselves, independent of direct communication with God. As a result, we do not hear His voice daily and we end up "having a form of godliness but denying its power" (2 Tim. 3:5).

WORDS FROM WESLEY

Hebrews 3:7–8

You have therefore good reason to believe, He is not only able, but willing to do this; to cleanse you from all your filthiness of flesh and spirit; to "save you from all your uncleannesses." This is the thing which you now long for; this is the faith which you now particularly need, namely, that the Great Physician, the lover of my soul, is willing to make me clean. But is He willing to do this tomorrow or today? Let Him answer for himself: "Today, if ye will hear" my "voice, harden not your hearts." If you put it off till tomorrow, you harden your hearts; you refuse to hear His voice. Believe, therefore, that He is willing to save you today. He is willing to save you *now*. "Behold, now is the accepted time." He now saith, "Be thou clean!" Only believe, and you also will immediately find, "all things are possible to him that believeth." Continue to believe in Him that loved thee, and gave himself for thee; that bore all thy sins in His own body on the tree; and He saveth thee from all condemnation, by His blood continually applied. (WJW, vol. 5, 166–167)

The result is that people end up coming to and serving in the church, but that is the extent of their faith. It is all in what they do, and what they do is a neat and organized part of their lives. It is a compartmentalized faith, a controlled faith. Anyone who approaches a friendship or marriage like this is doomed to disaster. We cannot control other people. We must learn to relate to them and allow the relationship to be dynamic and constantly developing. New things constantly arise in healthy relationships. It is a distinctive of relationships.

WORDS FROM WESLEY

Hebrews 3:9

When your fathers—That hard-hearted and stiff-necked generation. So little cause had their descendants to glory in them, *tempted me*—Whether I could and would help them: *proved me*—Put my patience to the proof, even while they saw my glorious works, both of judgment and mercy, and that for forty years. (ENNT)

If we know God personally, if we hear His voice, then we have no need for signs, wonders, or checklists of goodness. We can move at His prompting; talk to our neighbors about Jesus; give away material items we don't need; reject ambition for money, fame, and power. God calls us to go into the highways and hedges, welcome the outcasts of society, and befriend the oppressed. The rich young ruler turned away from Jesus because he valued his wealth more than discovering how to live in communion with God and others. God calls us to be selfless, to be self-sacrificial. Many times we decide what that means for us, and usually it is quite comfortable. When God speaks, He may well call us into a desert or ask us to do something that seems gigantic to us. After departing Egypt, the Hebrews were afraid to enter the Promised Land because the people living there were physically imposing. They hardened their hearts by trusting in what they could see rather than being confident in what they could not see. They traded the rest and peace of God for forty years of wandering in the desert. Unless we seek God's voice and act upon what we hear, regardless of what we see, we too will trade His rest for a lifetime of stress.

Christianity Is a Relationship with Others (Heb. 3:12–19)

John Wesley said there is no such holiness as solitary holiness. In other words, we cannot be Christians by ourselves. Sin is too powerful. We will be overcome. We have a responsibility to watch over the lives of one another. We cannot assume that anyone among us is immune to **sin's deceitfulness** (v. 13). Verse 16 reminds us that those who rebelled were the very ones who witnessed God part the Red Sea and save them from Pharaoh's army. We do no one any favors by placing them on a spiritual pedestal. In fact, we may put them at risk. Remember the saying, "familiarity breeds contempt." We must be careful that our familiarity with God and the church does not lull us into a false sense of security in which we begin to rationalize our wishes and desires as the will of God. This means we need to pray for the saints of the church just as diligently as we pray for the salvation of those outside the church, for an unbelieving heart is a self-centered heart, and self-centeredness is a constant threat.

What was **their unbelief** as the author described those who were unable to enter God's rest in verse 19? It was their refusal to act upon the promise of God. Under the old covenant the promise entailed an inheritance of land with physical, geographical boundaries. This implied that God would supply all their needs, water being essential to a desert people. Over and over, the Israelites failed to act on God's promise to supply their basic needs and, instead, they tried to be self-sufficient and complained against God for His apparent lack of faithfulness.

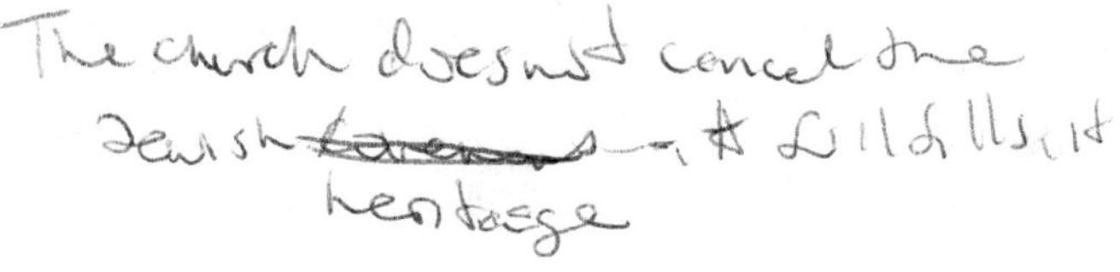

WORDS FROM WESLEY

Hebrews 3:12

Take heed lest there be in any of you—As there was in them: *an evil heart of unbelief*—Unbelief is the parent of all evil, and the very essence of unbelief lies, in departing from God, as the *living God*—The fountain of all our life, holiness, happiness. (ENNT)

The new covenant promise is an inheritance of an eternal land where there is no death and disease, no crying or pain. The old covenant required battle with greater forces. The new covenant requires loving where there is no love given in return. Both are based on God's promise that faithfulness to the covenant will bring rest and peace. Neither is evident to the human eye. Both assail the self-centeredness of sinful humanity. Both require a collective effort of all those who believe.

Selfless love requires us to believe that God will supply our basic needs. This frees us from the worries of life that we may live for others. This is faith. This is God's rest. This is how we live for and in today. May God bless the study of His promise. Today if you hear His voice, may you act and not harden your heart.

DISCUSSION

Life is full of distractions, even in the church, but the author of Hebrews made it clear that the way to strengthen your faith is to keep your eyes on Jesus.

1. What do you think it means to "fix your thoughts on Jesus" (Heb. 3:1)?

2. Why is Jesus "worthy of greater honor than Moses" (v. 3)?

3. How do you define God's house?

4. How does a person enter into a saving relationship with God?

5. What help do you find in verses 12–15 for strengthening your relationship with God?

6. What, if anything, might be threatening your relationship with God? What will you do to remove that threat?

7. What is the best thing you can do to help a fellow believer fix his or her eyes on Jesus?

8. How does the hope of heaven help you stay close to Jesus?

PRAYER

Lord, keep our hearts soft, so that we might not drift away as those who did so in the wilderness. Remind us to constantly look for opportunities to encourage others in the faith.

4

FAITH—THE KEY TO ENTERING GOD'S REST

Hebrews 4:1–16

Make every effort to enter God's rest through faith in Jesus Christ.

Consistent, adequate sleep may be as important to good health as proper diet and exercise. It allows the body to rebuild, relax, and refresh. Stress and anxiety do not trouble the heart and mind during sound, restful sleep. Further, a good sleep pattern may help to prolong life for cancer patients. The Cancer Prevention Study II of the American Cancer Society followed more than a million participants for six years. The best survival rate was found among those who slept about seven hours a night, the worst among those who slept less than four-and-a-half hours.

This study inspires us to enjoy the spiritual rest God offers His people. This rest lets us cast aside our anxieties and approach the throne of grace confidently.

COMMENTARY

The book of Hebrews is a beautifully crafted sermon that is masterfully designed to teach and encourage the Christians to whom it was sent. We do not know for sure who the author of the book was or the exact date of its composition. However, the rich biblical exposition and soul-stirring challenges of this writer are as relevant for us today as they were nearly two thousand years ago. Most likely this sermon was written in the latter half of the first century and sent as a letter to a house church made up of Christians from a Jewish background, possibly living in the area of Rome. It seems they had grown discouraged and were tempted to turn back from following Christ to the comfort and familiarity of Judaism. Since Judaism was an approved religion in the Roman Empire, they could avoid the Roman persecution that had or was soon to plague the Christian community. They could also evade the shame and ridicule heaped upon them by friends and family who did not understand why they would follow this new way of Christianity.

The passionate, pastoral heart of the author came through clearly as he did his best to motivate and encourage his audience to persevere in following Christ and "hold firmly to the faith we profess" (4:14). His sermon is a combination of alternating sections that explain passages from the Old Testament and sections that strongly exhort them to continue on the pilgrimage they had begun toward the heavenly city. The central purpose of this sermon was to cause the listeners to understand the superiority of Jesus Christ and the sufficient provision He has made that enabled them to enjoy fellowship with God and lead faithful lives, ultimately joining Him and all the heroes of the faith in the heavenly homeland forever.

Chapter 4 comes at the conclusion of the opening section (1:1—4:13) of this book, which demonstrates the superiority of the Son's message over the former revelation that came through the prophets and the angels, as well as His supremacy over the great leader of God's people, Moses the lawgiver. Verses 14–16 are a bridge leading us into the central section of this book (4:14—10:31), which describes this great high priest, Jesus Christ, and the perfect sacrifice He has made on our behalf. Chapter 4 progresses from the warning and encouragement not to fail to enter God's rest (vv. 1–11) to the reality of our complete exposure before the living Word (vv. 12–13) and concludes with the wonderful hope of our great High Priest (vv. 14–16). He has provided all the resources we need to enter God's rest and successfully pass examination before digging into the Word of God.

The Danger of Failing to Enter God's Rest (Heb. 4:1–5)

In the preceding section (3:7–19), the writer used Psalm 95:7–11 to show his listeners the danger of failing to believe and obey God. The psalmist referred to the events of Numbers 13–14 in which the children of Israel failed to enter the Promised Land of Canaan. Instead, they doubted God's ability to lead them victoriously against the land's inhabitants and rebelled against the leadership of Moses and Aaron. They are often referred to as the "wilderness generation" because their disobedience resulted in their deaths in the wilderness instead of entering the land of security and rest. The recipients of the letter to the Hebrews would have known Psalm 95 from worship, so the writer used it to set up a sharp contrast between those who obey and enter God's rest and those who do not.

WORDS FROM WESLEY

Hebrews 4:1

"Having therefore these promises, dearly beloved," both in the Law and in the Prophets, and having the prophetic word confirmed unto us in the gospel, by our blessed Lord and His apostles; "let us cleanse ourselves from all filthiness of flesh and spirit, perfecting holiness in the fear of God." "Let us fear, lest" so many "promises being made us of entering into his rest," which He that hath entered into, has ceased from His own works, "any of us should come short of it." "This one thing let us do, forgetting those things which are behind, and reaching forth unto those things which are before, let us press toward the mark, for the prize of the high calling of God in Christ Jesus;" crying unto Him day and night, till we also are "delivered from the bondage of corruption, into the glorious liberty of the sons of God!" (WJW, vol. 6, 19)

The promise of entering his rest still stands (Heb. 4:1), but they must **be careful** not to end up like the wilderness generation. They should not give in to the same disobedience and failure. The

NASB captures the importance of the first phrase of this verse by following it with "let us fear" (rather than the NIV's "let us be careful). The danger was that, after hearing the gospel, they would be like **those who heard** that message but **did not combine it with faith** (v. 2). The result of this failure was God's pronouncement from Psalm 95:11: **"So I declared on oath in my anger, 'They shall never enter my rest'"** (Heb. 4:3). It is not enough to just hear the Word; hearers must receive it in obedient faith and become doers of the Word (compare James 1:22–25).

This is the first time **faith** (Heb. 4:2) appears in the book of Hebrews, and it will reappear numerous times, especially in chapter 11. In this context, obedience is faith in action, as God's people are called to live as if God's power is real in the present and His promises for the future are certain. This life of active faith is the opposite of the wilderness generation's tragic example and ends in a completely different result, for **we who have believed enter that rest** (Heb. 4:3).

In verse 4, the writer returned to the Old Testament to prove his point. Since Psalm 95 revealed that this rest is God's rest, he took his listeners to the natural place in the Old Testament where an explanation was offered of what God's rest looks like. Here he interpreted the Scriptures using a rabbinic technique known as "verbal analogy." Since the noun *rest* in Psalm 95:11 is from the same word family as the verb *rested* in Genesis 2:2, he associated these two passages to demonstrate that God's **work has been finished since the creation of the world** (Heb. 4:3). Consequently, this rest is patterned after the rest God himself entered into after finishing His work of creation. In the next section, the author stressed the importance for his hearers to properly respond to this rest.

The Command to Enter God's Rest Today (Heb. 4:6–11)

The rest that the Israelites forfeited **because of their disobedience** is still offered to those who respond in faith, and **it still remains that some will enter that rest** (v. 6). The writer again quoted from Psalm 95, this time directing his audience to focus on the word *today* (Ps. 95:7–8). **Today, if you hear his voice, do not harden your hearts** (Heb. 4:7). Anticipating the response that this promise referred to Canaan and was fulfilled when the next generation finally entered the land, he countered that **if Joshua had given them rest, God would not have spoken later about another day** (v. 8). In other words, the rest promised by God through David could not have been the rest Joshua had already given Israel. Thus, this important message of warning and encouragement was urged upon the Hebrews as a present-tense reality.

WORDS FROM WESLEY

Hebrews 4:11

Now, then, "strive to enter in at the strait gate," being penetrated with the deepest sense of the inexpressible danger your soul is in, so long as you are in a broad way—so long as you are void of poverty of spirit, and all that inward religion, which the many, the rich, the wise, account madness. "Strive to enter in"; being pierced with sorrow and shame for having so long run on with the unthinking crowd, utterly neglecting, if not despising, that "holiness without which no man can see the Lord." Strive, as in an agony of holy fear, lest "a promise being made you of entering into his rest," even that "rest which remaineth for the people of God," you should nevertheless "come short of it." Strive, in all the fervour of desire, with "groanings which cannot be uttered. Strive by prayer without ceasing; at all times, in all places, lifting up your heart to God, and giving him no rest, till you. "awake up after his likeness," and are "satisfied with it." (WJW, vol. 6, 412–413)

The writer concluded: **There remains, then, a Sabbath-rest for the people of God; for anyone who enters God's rest also rests from his own work, just as God did from his** (vv. 9–10). In combination with the earlier reference to God's rest after completing creation (v. 4), we can see that this rest the Hebrews are to enter into is based on the pattern of God's own rest and characterized by ceasing to seek after our own way and designs. Instead, the writer urged his audience to turn to God's plan for them with faithful and obedient hearts that are submissive to His will.

Ironically, they must **make every effort to enter** this resting, yielded fellowship with God (v. 11). Rather than **following their example of disobedience**, the Hebrews (and we) are to demonstrate the faith that the wilderness generation should have modeled, and must diligently strive to be both hearers and faithful doers of the Word of God.

Finally, the writer was concerned in verses 1–11 that all members of the community enter this rest and do their best to help those around them do the same. The Greek phrases in verse 1 ("that none of you be found to have fallen short") and verse 11 (**that no one will fall**) alert us to the fact that every individual is important. We must be concerned with the spiritual conditions of our Christian brothers and sisters and do our best to encourage them to faithfully and obediently persevere in following Christ and entering God's promised rest.

The Penetrating Word of God (Heb. 4:12–13)

These verses are an appropriate closing to the first major division of the book, which began with the announcement of God's speaking in these last days by His Son (1:1–2). The same Greek word is used for this **word of God** (4:12) as was used for the message the wilderness generation rejected in verse 2. However, this **word of God** is still **living and active** today, penetrating to the very depths of our being. It exposes even the motives behind our actions as **it judges the thoughts and attitudes of the heart** (v. 12). No one is exempt from this examination, since **nothing in all creation is hidden from God's sight** (v. 13; compare Ps. 139). This fact of God's completely accurate, all-encompassing, inescapable knowledge of our actions and intentions is either the best or worst news we could ever hear. For those who respond to the Word with faith and obediently enter into God's rest, there is the assurance that God sees and knows the hearts that are turned toward Him. But for those who foolishly follow the example of the wilderness generation, there is the assurance that nothing can be hidden from God, and He will ultimately call them to **give account** (v. 13) for their response to His Word.

WORDS FROM WESLEY

Hebrews 4:12

For the word of God—Preached, ver. 2 and armed with threatenings, ver. 3 *is living and powerful*—Attended with the power of the living God, and conveying either life or death to the hearers; *sharper than any two-edged sword*—Penetrating the heart more than this does the body: *piercing*—Quite through, and laying open, *the soul and spirit, joints and marrow*—The inmost recesses of the mind, which the apostle beautifully and strongly expresses by this heap of figurative words: *and is a discerner*—Not only of *the thoughts*—But also of the *intentions*. (ENNT)

Our Great High Priest (Heb. 4:14–16)

These final verses introduce the section of Hebrews (4:14—10:31) that describes our great High Priest, Jesus Christ, and His ministry. The power of His effective sacrifice provides the resources we need to do our part and enter into God's rest. These verses are also a bridge leading us from the discussion of God's word spoken through His Son (1:1—4:13) to the next part of the book, which describes the content of that revelation.

The writer stressed the fact that **we have a great high priest** (v. 14); as we will see in chapter 5, this High Priest is unlike any other high priest who ever served in the temple. He **has gone**

through the heavens into the very presence of God. Because of this reality, we are to **hold firmly to the faith we profess** (v. 14).

Following this exhortation, the writer provided a further description of this great High Priest. He is not **unable to sympathize with our weaknesses**; instead, he **has been tempted in every way, just as we are** (v. 15). When Jesus Christ lived among us, He experienced the temptations, pains, and trials that are part of what it means to be a human being in a fallen world. He knows what we are going through in our day-to-day struggles. However, the writer added a vitally important qualification: Jesus **was without sin** (v. 15). This fact sets this great High Priest apart from all other high priests.

WORDS FROM WESLEY

Hebrews 4:13

In his sight—It is God, whose word is thus *powerful*: It is God, *in* whose *sight* every creature is *manifest:* and of this His word working on the conscience, gives the fullest conviction; *but all things are naked and opened*—Plainly alluding to the sacrifices under the law, which were first flayed, and then (as the Greek word literally means) *cleft asunder through the neck* and back-bone: so that every thing both without and within, was exposed to open view. (ENNT)

Because of this, the writer urged his listeners to **approach the throne of grace with confidence** (v. 16). This chapter that began with an exhortation to enter God's rest ends with the reason why we can do so: We have a great High Priest who knows what it is like to be human, has lived a sinless life, and has provided all of the resources we need to hear and obey God's voice. Because of Him, **we may receive mercy and find grace to help us in our time of need** (v. 16). This summary of the writer's message about our great High Priest presented in verses 14–16 captures the heart of his entire sermon.

DISCUSSION

In a world where stress, fear, and anxiety seem to be the norm, Jesus invites us to come to Him to find rest for our souls. Hebrews compels us to find rest by continuing in faith.

1. Why didn't the Israelites in the wilderness enter into God's rest (Heb. 4:2, 6)?

2. How do you know life in Canaan was not the ultimate rest God had promised?

3. How do you know we cannot enter God's rest by performing good works (v. 10)?

4. How does verse 12 complement the truth that God looks at the heart?

5. Why are pure motives and attitudes so important in what we say and do?

6. Why is it futile to pretend to be God's follower (v. 13)?

7. Find in verses 14–15 several facts about our great High Priest Jesus that distinguish Him from all the other high priests in Israel's history.

8. When you pray, how confident are you that your deepest needs will be met? What truths in verses 14–15 boost your confidence?

PRAYER

Lord, thank You for the Bible which is able to pierce through any pretense. Thank You for a Savior who can empathize with any trial we may be experiencing.

5

JESUS MEETS THE QUALIFICATIONS

Hebrews 5:1–14

Jesus is uniquely qualified to be our high priest.

Unless an adult's digestive system can handle only baby food, adults choose to eat food they can sink their teeth into, chew, and mash. After a hard day of work, who wants to pop a tiny jar of strained veggies prepared for babies and spoon it into his or her mouth glob by glob? Steak and potatoes might seem much more tantalizing and appetizing.

Believers who choose to stay with a diet of elementary truths long after their conversion are like adults stuck on baby food. They need to progress from milk and soft food to solid food. They will not become mature believers until they sink their teeth into the meat of the Word.

This study motivates us to become mature believers.

COMMENTARY

The author of the book of Hebrews continued in chapter 5 with a mix of exposition of Old Testament Scriptures and exhortation to warn and encourage the people to whom he was writing. He moved from discussing God's Word spoken through His Son in 1:1—4:13 to the heart of the book of Hebrews, which describes the ministry of Jesus Christ in 4:14—10:31. The bridge into this section occurs in 4:14–16, where he discussed the resources provided for his audience by their great High Priest, Jesus the Son of God. He began to explain the high priesthood of Jesus, starting in 5:1–10 with a comparison and contrast between His ministry and the ministry of the high priests who were descendents of Aaron.

In the development of verses 1–10, the writer used a carefully constructed literary device called a *chiasmus* to describe the two high priesthoods he was comparing and contrasting. Thus, his first and last points correspond, his second and second to last points are related, and so on. This organized his discussion and made it easier for his audience to remember. It also focused their attention on the center section (vv. 4–6). The five elements of correspondence in this *chiasmus* are: (1) the high priesthood of Aaron and the high priesthood of the Son (vv. 1, 10); (2) their high priestly ministries (vv. 2, 9); (3) their humanity (vv. 2, 8); (4) their sacrifices (vv. 3, 7); and (5) their appointments as high priests (vv. 4, 5–6).

The remainder of the chapter (vv. 11–14) is the beginning of an exhortation concerning the problem of spiritual immaturity.

A Mortal, Sinful High Priest (Heb. 5:1–4)

We must not let the chapter divisions in our English Bibles cause us to forget the relationship between 4:14–16 and 5:1–10. The writer introduced the great High Priest, Jesus, to his audience, and then contrasted this great High Priest with the mortal high priests who descended from the line of Aaron, the first high priest of Israel.

In verse 1, we find that **every high priest** must be **selected from among men and . . . appointed to represent them in matters related to God**. Thus, he must be chosen as a representative of his fellow human beings; it is the job of the high priest to stand before God on their behalf. On the Day of Atonement (Lev. 16), he would enter the Most Holy Place and offer a sacrifice to make atonement for the people. There were also other times during the year in which he would **offer gifts and sacrifices for sins** (Heb. 5:1).

This Aaronic high priest was **able to deal gently** and compassionately **with those** he represented because **he himself** was **subject to weakness** (v. 2) in the same way they were. On the Day of Atonement, the high priest was required to make atonement for himself before he could represent the people. Because he also was **subject to weaknesses** (v. 2), **he** had **to offer sacrifices for his own sins, as well as for the sins of the people** (v. 3).

It should be pointed out that verse 2 describes the people he was making atonement for as **those who are ignorant and are going astray**. Under the Old Testament's sacrificial system, the priests were required to offer sacrifices for sins committed unintentionally or those that were not explicitly premeditated. The high priests were held to a high standard of holiness before God with even stricter regulations than those laid upon ordinary priests. They could not live in defiant rebellion against God; however, these men were still fallible human beings and needed atonement.

Finally, like their ancestor Aaron, these priests had to **be called by God** (v. 4). The priesthood was an important position, and **no one** took **this honor upon himself**. It was only bestowed upon a man who was appointed **by God** in accordance with the conditions God himself had established.

Next the writer turned to a comparison and contrast of this mortal, sinful high priest with the eternal, obedient High Priest, who was the focus of his entire sermon.

An Eternal, Obedient High Priest (Heb. 5:5–10)

In the structure of the *chiasmus* the preacher was using, his audience's attention was drawn in this central comparison in verses 4–6, to the position of authority given to those high priests who were appointed by God. Even the **Christ . . . did not take upon himself the glory of becoming a high priest** (v. 5). Instead, the author of Hebrews again returned to the Old Testament to demonstrate that He was appointed to this role of high priest by His Father. In verse 5, the preacher quoted Psalm 2:7, which he used at the beginning of his sermon to establish the divine Sonship of Jesus (Heb. 1:5). Also quoted is Psalm 110:4, where God instituted Christ as High Priest with the words, **"You are a priest forever, in the order of Melchizedek"** (Heb. 5:6). (The relationship between Jesus and Melchizedek will be further explored in Heb. 7.) The preacher uses these two Old Testament quotations to tie together the Sonship and the priesthood of Jesus Christ. These two aspects have already been discussed independently (1:1–14; 2:16–18), but now we understand that they are inseparably linked and His high priesthood is effective because He is the Son of God. Building upon the superiority of the Son, which was seen in the first part of the book, we now find an incomparably superior High Priest who has been appointed to a position of unequaled authority.

WORDS FROM WESLEY

Hebrews 5:7

Who in the days of his flesh—Those two days in particular, wherein His sufferings were at the height, *having offered up prayers and supplications*—Thrice, *with strong crying and tears*—In the garden, *to him that was able to save him from death*—Which yet He endured, in obedience to the will of His Father, *and being heard in that which he* particularly *feared*—When the cup was offered Him first, there was set before Him that horrible image of a painful, shameful, accursed death, which moved Him to pray conditionally against it: for if He had desired it, His heavenly Father would have sent Him more than twelve legions of angels to have delivered Him. But what He most exceedinlgy feared was, the weight of infinite justice; the being bruised and put to grief by the hand of God himself. Compared with this, every thing else was a mere nothing. (ENNT)

The preacher then turned his focus to the ministry of the Son during His **life on earth** (5:7). Perhaps referring to Jesus' prayer to His Father in the garden of Gethsemane, he said **he offered up prayers and petitions with loud cries and tears to the one who could save him from death, and he was heard because of his reverent submission** (v. 7). We see that although the Son willingly submitted to death on the cross in order to carry out His high priestly ministry, through His subsequent resurrection and exaltation to the right hand of the Father, He was indeed rescued from the power of death and now He triumphantly holds the keys of death and the grave (Rev. 1:18)!

Just as the Aaronic high priest could identify with the people he represented, Jesus, **although he was a son . . . learned obedience from what he suffered** (Heb. 5:8). Even though this High Priest was exalted to the highest level of authority and prominence as the Son, He subjected himself to suffering during His life on earth, and lived out a pattern of obedient submission to the will of His Father, climaxing with His death on the cross. He learned obedience by being the paramount example of a life completely surrendered to doing the will of God. Unlike the Aaronic high priests, He never sinned (compare 4:15) or disobeyed His Father in any way; thus, His ministry was infinitely more effective than theirs.

Because of this life of complete obedience, Jesus was **made perfect** and **became the source of eternal salvation for all who obey him** (5:9). Here we see the strongest discontinuity between the effects of the Aaronic high priesthood and Jesus'. While they could only "deal gently" with sinners because they themselves were also "subject to weakness" (v. 2), Jesus is able to provide **eternal salvation for all who obey him** (v. 9). Any power that the Aaronic priesthood's often-repeated sacrifices had to atone for sin was provided through the once and for all sacrifice of the Son's obedient life and death. Jesus was made perfect, or complete, in the sense that He lived an obedient life and made an effective sacrifice that provides complete atonement for sin. The present active tense of the verb **obey** in verse 9 indicates that this eternal salvation is only available to those who continuously and consistently live a life modeled after the Son's complete submission to the will of His Father.

WORDS FROM WESLEY

Hebrews 5:9

It is a vain thought which some have entertained, that death will put an end to the soul as well as the body: It will put an end to neither the one nor the other; it will only alter the manner of their existence. But when the body "returns to the dust as it was, the spirit will return to God that gave it." Therefore, at the moment of death, it must be unspeakably happy, or unspeakably miserable. (WJW, vol. 6, 195)

This section closes with a reaffirmation of God's appointment of the Son to a superior position of authority as a **high priest in the order of Melchizedek** (v. 10). This order was an eternal priesthood that vastly surpassed the limited ministries of the mortal, Aaronic high priests (compare 7:1–28).

The writer more fully explained the high priesthood of Jesus Christ throughout the rest of his sermon. However, he first turned his attention to a matter that could have prevented his listeners from understanding what he wanted to say. He addressed the problem of their spiritual immaturity and called them to a higher level.

The Problem of Spiritual Immaturity (Heb. 5:11–14)

Verses 11–14 begin an exhortation concerning the negative effects of spiritual immaturity; this section continues until 6:8. The author had **much to say about this** great High Priest and His ministry, but it was **hard to explain because** his audience was **slow to learn** (5:11). This last phrase can literally be translated "dull of hearing" (KJV, NASB). Just as a person with a physical hearing handicap might struggle to hear the speech of others and even mishear or fail to understand important portions of conversations, the writer was impeded in his explanation because of the "spiritually hard-of-hearing" condition of his listeners. The fact that they were berated for this hearing problem shows there was something they could do about it. They fell into this condition because of their neglect to quickly and obediently act on what they had heard.

Although they **ought to be teachers** themselves, instead it was necessary for **someone** else **to teach** them **the elementary truths of God's word all over again** (v. 12). They were compared to infants who **need milk, not solid food** (v. 12). This solid food is the **teaching about righteousness** (v. 13), which includes the instruction about Jesus' high priestly ministry and the benefits it entails for obedient believers. This teaching comes from the Word of God as it has been revealed through the Son.

WORDS FROM WESLEY

Hebrews 5:14

But strong meat—Those sublimer truths relating to *perfection* (ch. 6:1) *belong to them of full age who by habit—Habit* here signifies, strength of spiritual understanding, arising from maturity of spiritual age: by, or in consequence of this habit, they exercise themselves in these things, with ease, readiness, cheerfulness and profit. (ENNT)

In verse 14, the preacher revealed to his audience how this condition of spiritual immaturity might be avoided or remedied. The **solid food** that was vitally needed for them to grow and develop as they should **is for the mature, who by constant use have trained themselves to distinguish good from evil** (v. 14).

The spiritual discernment of the believer concerning what is good or evil must be exercised faithfully for the person to make choices that please God. As Christians regularly give their spiritual discernment a workout, they participate in a "circle of maturity." That is, faithfully listening to God's Word and obeying Him leads to further spiritual development and deeper understanding of God's Word. This deepened understanding then allows one to hear more clearly God's voice and live a life of submissive obedience. This process of growth and development enables the believer to live in a way that increasingly resembles the example of our eternal, obedient High Priest, who lived a life of "reverent submission" to His Father's will (5:7) and is now "the source of eternal salvation for all who obey him" (v. 9).

DISCUSSION

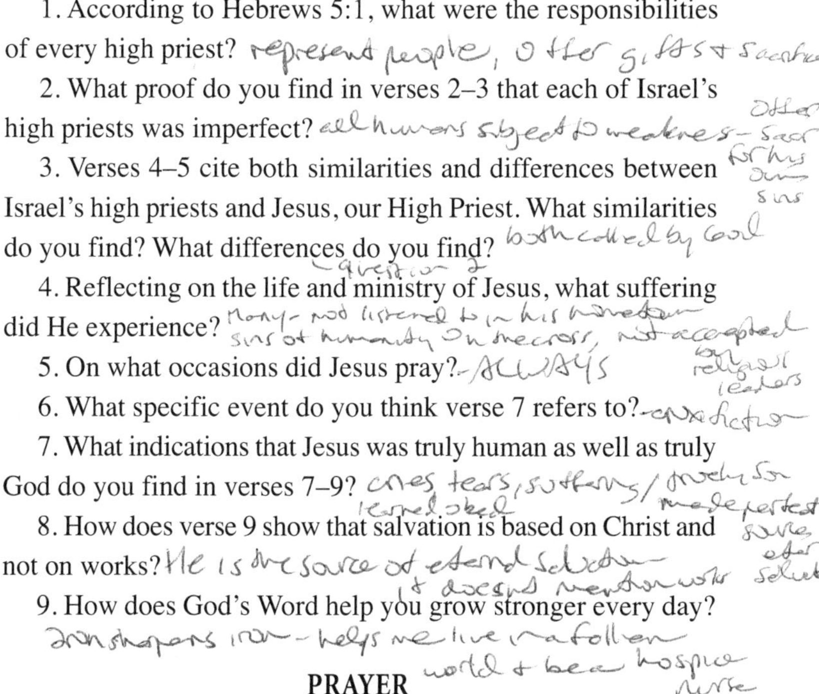

Christians sometimes want to know what the "minimum qualifications" are for faith. But Hebrews tells us it's essential to grow into maturity in Christ.

1. According to Hebrews 5:1, what were the responsibilities of every high priest?
2. What proof do you find in verses 2–3 that each of Israel's high priests was imperfect?
3. Verses 4–5 cite both similarities and differences between Israel's high priests and Jesus, our High Priest. What similarities do you find? What differences do you find?
4. Reflecting on the life and ministry of Jesus, what suffering did He experience?
5. On what occasions did Jesus pray?
6. What specific event do you think verse 7 refers to?
7. What indications that Jesus was truly human as well as truly God do you find in verses 7–9?
8. How does verse 9 show that salvation is based on Christ and not on works?
9. How does God's Word help you grow stronger every day?

PRAYER

Lord, teach us to learn obedience through suffering, just as Jesus did. Increase our confidence that You use everything in our lives, even our trials and tribulations; You waste nothing.

6

PURSUING PERFECTION

Hebrews 6:1–20

Christian perfection is a lifelong pursuit in full cooperation with God.

Ron, a retired high school history teacher, maintains a website that promotes atheism. But he hasn't always been an atheist. As a matter of fact, he used to profess to be a believer. He grew up espousing biblical truth, and in his youth, he graduated from a Bible college. His classmates admired his devotion to Christ and his ability to teach Sunday school children successfully. His friends say Ron's departure from the faith occurred after Bible college, when he studied education at a secular university.

One thing is clear: Ron chose to fall away.

This study inspires us to choose *not* to fall away, but to go on to maturity in Christ.

COMMENTARY

The author of Hebrews wrote to show that "Christ is better." In 1:1–4, he declared Christ to be better than the prophets. In chapters 1–7, he showed Christ to be better than other mediators: better than angels (1:5—2:18), better than Moses (3:1—4:13), and better than Aaron (4:14—7:28). In this latter section, he declared Christ to be a sympathetic High Priest (4:14–16) and a perfect High Priest (5:1–10). In Hebrews 5:6, the author quoted from Psalm 110:4, saying our Lord is "a priest forever, in the order of Melchizedek." And then in 5:10, he declared that Christ "was designated by God to be high priest in the order of Melchizedek." But then he stepped aside from that discussion and did not return to it again until 6:20 and 7:1.

The material between 5:10 and 7:1 is one of several digressions or interludes from the main discussion, which is more theological in nature. These interludes are given to practical exhortations. (For the other interludes, see 2:1–4; 3:7–19; 4:11–16; 10:19–39; 12:25–29; 13:9–16.) In 5:11—6:20, the author expressed a deep pastoral concern for the Hebrew Christians to whom he was writing. He was fearful that their slowness to grow and mature in Christ may have hindered them in understanding what he would say about Christ as a high priest in the order of Melchizedek. And beginning with Hebrews 6, he exhorted them to "go on to maturity" (v. 1). He warned them of possible irrevocable loss if they did not. He assured them that this did not have to happen. And he exhorted them to pursue a "maturity," "perfection" (KJV), or completeness anchored in the love of Jesus.

The Need to Go On (Heb. 6:1–3)

The author had called his readers to task for their spiritual immaturity; they had been Christians long enough that they should have been teaching others (Heb. 5:11–14). Then he told them what they were to leave and what they were to go on to. They were to **leave the elementary teachings about Christ** (6:1). Three pairs of **elementary teachings** are listed. Some scholars have thought these were familiar elements from Judaism, which foreshadowed or pointed forward to the Christian gospel. These needed to be left behind for the Hebrews to really become Christians. Other scholars have thought the elementary teachings were matters taught to new converts at the beginning of their Christian experience in a kind of catechism. These introductory truths needed to left behind to go on to the deeper truths of the gospel. The fact that the elementary teachings were about Christ tends to establish the second interpretation. The writer to the Hebrews spoke of these as the foundation that does not need to be, nor should it be, laid **again** (v. 1). It was time to grow up, to **go on**

to maturity or "perfection" (KJV). The words used for "perfect" and "perfection" in the New Testament refer to wholeness, completeness—everything in that should be in, and nothing that shouldn't. John spoke repeatedly of love made perfect or complete (1 John 4:12, 17–18).

WORDS FROM WESLEY

Hebrews 6:1

What is then the perfection of which man is capable while he dwells in a corruptible body? It is the complying with that kind command, "My son, give me thy heart." It is the "loving the Lord his God with all his heart, and with all his soul, and with all his mind." This is the sum of Christian perfection: It is all comprised in that one word, Love. The first branch of it is the love of God: And as he that loves God loves his brother also, it is inseparably connected with the second: "Thou shalt love thy neighbour as thyself:" Thou shalt love every man as thy own soul, as Christ loved us. "On these two commandments hang all the Law and the Prophets:" These contain the whole of Christian perfection.

Another view of this is given us in those words of the great apostle: "Let this mind be in you which was also in Christ Jesus." For although this immediately and directly refers to the humility of our Lord, yet it may be taken in a far more extensive sense, so as to include the whole disposition of His mind, all His affections, all His tempers, both toward God and man. Now, it is certain that as there was no evil affection in Him, so no good affection or temper was wanting. So that "whatsoever things are holy, whatsoever things are lovely," are all included in "the mind that was in Christ Jesus." (WJW, vol. 6, 413)

The first pair of elementary teachings is **repentance from acts that lead to death, and of faith in God** (Heb. 6:1). **Repentance** is not just being sorry for being caught, or even just a genuine sorrow because of sins committed. The word signifies a complete change of mind and a reversal of direction. Repentance is a significant emphasis in the Old Testament as God sought to transform His people. John the Baptist, Jesus, and the apostles repeatedly called for repentance in announcing the good news of salvation. It has always been the first response required of humans when turning to God. But it must be paired with faith in God. For the Jews, the Old Testament had virtually equated believing God with obeying God. For the Christian, this is a call to faith in His love and invitation, faith in His Son, whom the Father provided as our sacrifice.

The second pair of elementary teachings includes **instruction about baptisms** and **the laying on of hands** (v. 2). **Baptisms** could also be translated "washings." The Hebrews would be well-acquainted with the ceremonial washings of the Old Testament for cleansing from ceremonial uncleanness. And they performed a kind of baptism on Gentiles who converted to Judaism. For the Christians, baptism in water was the initiating ritual for those being added to the church. The plural form, **baptisms**, is unusual. However, John the Baptist talked about two baptisms—one in water and one in the Holy Spirit. Priscilla and Aquila in Acts 18:24–26 and Paul in Acts 19:1–6, taught about the differences between the two. Perhaps, in the catechism classes, converts were taught the differences. The **laying on of hands** (Heb. 6:2) was familiar from the Old Testament in the conferring of a blessing (Gen. 48:10–20), the offering of a sacrifice to God (Ex. 29:10), and in setting a person apart for an office or ministry (Num. 27:18–22; Deut. 34:9). In the New Testament church, this action was used to impart the gift of the Holy Spirit (Acts 8:17; 9:17–18), commission persons to service (6:3–6; 13:2–3), bring healing (28:8), and confer a blessing or spiritual gift (2 Tim. 1:6).

The third pair of elementary teachings spoke about matters yet to come: **the resurrection of the dead, and eternal judgment** (Heb. 6:2)—the one very promising, the other potentially very threatening. These were mostly just hinted at in the Old Testament, but **resurrection** and the final **judgment** were more fully developed in Judaism in the centuries between the Old Testament and the New Testament. In the teachings of Jesus and the apostles, they were strong emphases. They dealt with eternal destiny.

The Danger of Falling Away (Heb. 6:4–8)

In this passage, the writer to the Hebrews wrote some of the most solemn words in the New Testament. He spoke of persons thoroughly converted to Christ as indicated by five evidences: they had **once been enlightened**; they had **tasted the heavenly gift** (salvation); they had **shared in the Holy Spirit**; they had **tasted the goodness of the word of God** (both written and spoken); **and** they had **the powers of the coming age** (experiencing or performing miracles or mighty acts in the service of God) (vv. 4–5). This is not a description of persons with a shallow or superficial acquaintance with the gospel. The word **tasted** used here repeatedly also can be translated "partake of" or "enjoy." It was also used by this same writer with reference to Jesus' death on the cross, speaking in Hebrews 2:9 of His "tasting" (KJV) death. The persons referred to had been truly and fully converted.

If such persons fall away, **it is impossible for** them **to be brought back to repentance, because . . . they are crucifying the Son of God all over again** (6:4, 6). The falling away is not just a matter of spiritually slipping and falling. Forgiveness for that is readily available (1 John 2:1–2). It is not a mere stumbling or temporary backsliding. Falling away is an intentional, willful rejection of Christ after having known Him intimately. In effect, they are crucifying the Son of God all over again. The writer to the Hebrews said it is possible for believers, advanced in the faith, to willfully rebel, fall away, and be lost. If such is true of the mature, how much greater is the danger of those who cling to spiritual babyhood and fail to go on to maturity in Christ?

Does the writer mean to say there is no hope for truly and fully converted persons who fall away? The word translated **because** in Hebrews 6:6 can also be translated "while." Thus, it would mean that such persons could not be brought back to repentance *while* they were crucifying Christ again. If such persons would turn from their rebellion, repentance would still be possible. But the awful truth remains that willful and sustained rejection of the Savior after having a relationship with Him *can* lead to total and final lostness. The writer then illustrated the results from agriculture, as land producing good crops is blessed and land producing bad crops is cursed. This is not intended to teach that persons who serve the Lord well will be saved and those who serve Him poorly will be lost. Salvation is a matter of relationship rather than a matter of performance. But while the keeping is done by the Lord, the repentance and faith that first led the believer to salvation is to be continued as obedience and faith throughout this life.

WORDS FROM WESLEY

Hebrews 6:11

In how amiable a light do you now see the holy and perfect will of God! Now, therefore, labour that it may be fulfilled, both in you, by you, and upon you! Now watch and pray that you may sin no more, that you may see and shun the least transgression of His law! You see the motes which you could not see before, when the sun shines into a dark place. In like manner, you see the sins which you could not see before, now the Sun of Righteousness shines in your heart. Now then do all diligence to walk, in every respect, according to the light you have received! (WJW, vol. 5, 467)

Need for Faith and Patience (Heb. 6:9–12)

The writer hastened to say that he did not believe that his readers had fallen away so as to be without hope. **We are confident of better things in your case—things that accompany salvation** (v. 9). They had **shown** their **love** to **God** by helping and continuing to help **his people**. God would not forget their **love** or their

work (v. 10). But instead of tarrying in immaturity, they were **to show . . . diligence to the very end** (v. 11). They were not **to become lazy**. Rather, they were to **imitate** others **who through faith and patience** had inherited **what has been promised** (v. 12), making their **hope sure** (v. 11) or certain—faith in God who will always do His part, and for their part patience, persistence, steadfastness, endurance, pursuing the perfection or completeness available in Christ. The apostle Paul said on one occasion that he was "confident of this, that he who began a good work in you will carry it on to completion until the day of Christ Jesus" (Phil. 1:6). This is what the writer to the Hebrews was saying also.

WORDS FROM WESLEY

Hebrews 6:13

For—Ye have abundant encouragement, seeing no stronger promise could be made, than that great promise which God made to Abraham, and in him to us. (ENNT)

Our Anchor in Jesus (Heb. 6:13–20)

The writer to the Hebrews wanted to emphasize strongly the certainty of his readers' hope in Christ. So he turned to the Old Testament and cited their founding father, Abraham. He reminded his readers of God's promise to childless Abraham that he would have innumerable descendants, beginning with a son through Sarah (Gen. 12:1–3, 7; 13:14–17; 15:1–19; 17:1–22; 18:10–15; 22:15–18). And God had not stopped, even with seven promises. At the time of the last promise, God added to His **promise** (Heb. 6:13, which was guarantee enough) an **oath** (v. 16) to make it doubly sure. He said, "I swear by myself" (Gen. 22:16). The writer to the Hebrews pointed out that **men swear by someone greater than themselves, and the oath confirms what is said and**

puts an end to all argument (Heb. 6:16). There was no one greater than God for God to swear by, so He swore by himself. Thus, there should be no question about the certainty of the promise.

The writer to the Hebrews picked up on this. It was **because God wanted to make the unchanging nature of his purpose very clear** (v. 17). This was **so that, by two unchangeable things** (promise and oath) **in which it is impossible for God to lie, we who have fled to take hold of the hope offered to us may be greatly encouraged** (v. 18). This hope is **an anchor for the soul, firm and secure** (v. 19). But it is a most unusual anchor. Other anchors reach down through the watery depths to grasp something and hold tight. This one reaches up into heaven where the real temple is. **It enters the inner sanctuary**, the Most Holy Place, **behind the curtain** or veil, fastening itself in the place that most fully represents the reality and presence of God. Our hope can do so because Jesus, our High Priest, **has entered** there **on our behalf** (v. 20). He did so through His death. Our hope, our certainty, and our anchor were purchased by His love.

WORDS FROM WESLEY

Hebrews 6:17

God interposed by an oath—Amazing condescension! He who is greatest of all, acts as if He were a middle person, as if while He swears, He were less than himself, by whom He swears? Thou that hearest the promise, dost thou not yet believe? (ENNT)

DISCUSSION

Falling away from the faith is not something one must be anxious about, but it is something to guard against. And the best way to do that is to continue growing in Christ.

1. What elementary teachings do you find in Hebrews 6:1–3?

2. The writer to the Hebrews urged his readers to "go on to maturity" (v. 1). How would you define spiritual maturity?

3. Why do you agree or disagree that the persons referred to as falling away (v. 6) had been truly converted?

4. How would you define the falling away referred to in verse 6?

5. What evidence of genuine faith did the writer of Hebrews see in his readers' lives (vv. 9–10)?

6. How will you imitate those who demonstrated faith and patience (v. 12)?

7. What personal comfort and encouragement do you derive from the fact that God cannot lie (v. 18)?

8. On a scale of one to ten, how firm and secure do you believe your anchor of hope is today? How may you apply the truths given in Hebrews 6 to strengthen your hope?

PRAYER

Lord, teach us to desire growth; may we never become complacent in our faith. Spur us on to become more and more like Jesus every day.

7

DO WE NEED A HIGH PRIEST?

Hebrews 7:11–17, 25; 8:1–7

Jesus is the mediator of a new covenant.

Technology keeps advancing, and as it does, life changes—usually for the better. Cataract surgery used to require a hospital stay of several days, but technology has made it possible to recover on an outpatient basis. Typists used to cover errors with white-out. Today, the delete key performs the same function with less mess. Messages that once took days or weeks to arrive at their destination are now delivered within seconds of hitting the send button. It's hard to imagine reverting to a time before such technological advances.

The recipients of the letter to the Hebrews needed to understand that the new covenant and Jesus' priesthood were far superior to the old covenant and the former priesthood. This study inspires in us a deeper appreciation of what we have under the new covenant.

COMMENTARY

This study concludes the part of Hebrews that argues "Christ is better than other mediators" (chs. 1–7), and it brings to a climax the section showing that He is better than Aaron (4:14—7:28). It then begins the next part of Hebrews, which argues that "Christ provides a better covenant" (8:1—10:39). Chapter 8 shows that it is a better covenant because it is spiritual and inward.

The writer to the Hebrews first mentioned Melchizedek in 5:5. There he cited Psalm 110:4 and went on in Hebrews 5:10 to declare that that prophecy had been fulfilled in that Jesus "was designated by God to be high priest in the order of Melchizedek." But then he interrupted his theological discussion because he was fearful the Hebrews were lingering in spiritual babyhood and would find it difficult to understand (5:11–14). So he proceeded to exhort them to make their "hope sure" (6:11) and "to imitate those who through faith and patience inherit what has been promised" (6:12). He closed chapter 6 by saying again that Jesus "has become a high priest forever, in the order of Melchizedek" (6:20). He was then ready to resume his theological discussion.

In 7:1–10, the writer to the Hebrews summarized what little was known about Melchizedek from the Old Testament. He cited the story from Genesis 14 about a war between two alliances of kings, which led to the capture and removal of Abraham's nephew Lot and his family and possessions. Abraham and a band of his friends and servants defeated the kingly alliance that was responsible and rescued their captives. As Abraham was returning from this victory, Melchizedek came out to meet him (Gen. 14:18–20). He was referred to as "king of Salem" and as "priest of God Most High." His name means "king of righteousness." *Salem* may be a shortened form of Jerusalem, but it also means "peace." So this mysterious person who appeared so abruptly on the pages of sacred writing and quickly vanished again was both the "king of righteousness" and the "king of peace." While he apparently lived in the midst of the wicked and idolatrous Canaanites, he was the "priest of God Most High." In Genesis 14:22, Abraham referred to his own God as God Most High, indicating that Melchizedek served the true God. Contrary to the usual introduction of persons in Genesis, nothing is said about Melchizedek's ancestry, parents, birth, or death. But his greatness is shown by the fact that Abraham yielded to his blessing and paid tithes to him. The writer to the Hebrews pointed out that the lesser person is blessed by the greater person, so Melchizedek was greater than Abraham. And since the

Levites, Israel's appointed tithe collectors, were descendants of Abraham, they paid tithes to Melchizedek through Abraham, and Melchizedek was greater than the Levites and the priesthood derived from them.

Need for a Different Priestly Order (Heb. 7:11–17)

The writer to the Hebrews then used Melchizedek as a type or foreshadowing of Jesus. He quoted before from Psalm 110:4 and he did so again in 7:17. Psalm 110 is a messianic psalm. Verses 1–3 of that psalm spoke of the Messiah as a king established by the Lord (Yahweh). Jesus quoted from Psalm 110:1 and applied it to himself in one of His conversations with the Jewish religious leaders (Matt. 22:44). And Peter also quoted it at Pentecost, identifying Jesus with the second Lord (*Adonai*) spoken of there (Acts 2:34–36). The writer to the Hebrews cited Psalm 110:4 as predicting that the Messiah would also be **a priest forever in the order of Melchizedek** (Heb. 7:17).

The writer to the Hebrews then began to point out the deficiencies of the old priesthood and the superiority of the new. He declared that **if perfection could have been attained through the Levitical priesthood,** there would have been no **need for another priest to come** (v. 11). The **change of the priesthood** would also require **a change of the law** (v. 12). The old code of regulations was to be replaced with what James 2:8 calls the "royal law" of love (compare Matt. 5:43–45; John 13:34–35; 1 John 2:3–11). He called attention to the fact that Jesus was not from the tribe of Levi, but **from Judah** (Heb. 7:14), which had no relationship to the old priesthood. The old priesthood staked its claim on **ancestry**, but Jesus' claim was based on **the power of an indestructible life** (v. 16). The appearance of Melchizedek in Genesis without reference to a beginning or an ending made him a type of Jesus, who really did not have a beginning or an ending, but is eternal. While the writer did not develop the thought any further,

Melchizedek's identity as "king of righteousness" and "king of peace" also looked forward to Jesus as the Messiah. He was the true king of righteousness and peace (compare Isa. 9:6–7).

WORDS FROM WESLEY

Hebrews 7:15

And it is far more evident, that—Both the priesthood and the law are changed, because the priest now raised up, is not only of another tribe, but of a quite different order. (ENNT)

In Hebrews 7:18–24, the writer became more specific: The old way "was weak and useless" (v. 18); "the law made nothing perfect" (v. 19). Both in verses 11 and 19, the writer implied that a priesthood was needed that could perfectly or completely serve as the mediator between God and humans. He said that with the new priesthood, "a better hope is introduced, by which we draw near to God" (v. 19). And he pointed out that in Psalm 110:4, God had declared with an oath that the Messiah would be a priest forever. The old priesthood involved no oath; the new one is better because God doubly guaranteed it (compare Heb. 6:13–18). "Because of this oath, Jesus has become the guarantee of a better covenant" (7:22).

In 7:23–24, the writer pointed out that there has been a constantly recurring turnover in the old priesthood, because those priests were mortal and "death prevented them from continuing in office." But "Jesus lives forever," and therefore "he has a permanent priesthood."

Provision of a More-Effective Priest (Heb. 7:25)

The writer then declared that Jesus **is able to save completely those who come to God through him, because he always lives to intercede for them** (v. 25). The word translated **completely** is "to the uttermost" in the KJV. Some translators connect it to the time element and say that He is able to save forever. Probably both elements are intended. There is no aspect of sin Jesus cannot deal with and redeem us from, and He can do it forever. The Lord Jesus Christ can forgive past sins and He can cleanse us from the tendency to sin. He can break sinful habits and make sin distasteful to the transformed heart. And His ministry lasts **because he always lives to intercede for** us (v. 25; compare Rom. 8:26–27, 34).

WORDS FROM WESLEY

Hebrews 7:25

O do not take *any thing less than this* for the religion of Jesus Christ! Do not take part of it for the whole! What God hath joined together, put not asunder! Take no less for his religion, than the "faith that worketh by love;" all inward and outward holiness. Be not content with any religion which does not imply the destruction of all the works of the devil; that is, of all sin. We know, weakness of understanding, and a thousand infirmities, will remain, while this corruptible body remains; but sin need not remain: This is that work of the devil, eminently so called, which the Son of God was manifested to destroy in this present life. He is able, He is willing, to destroy it now, in all that believe in Him. Only be not straitened in your own bowels! Do not distrust His power, or His love! Put His promise to the proof! He hath spoken: And is He not ready likewise to perform? Only "come boldly to the throne of grace," trusting in His mercy; and you shall find, "He saveth to the uttermost all those that come to God through him!" (WJW, vol. 6, 276)

It is important to note that this complete, full, whole, lasting salvation is for those who come to God through Jesus. It is not for those who try to come by some other way. Jesus himself said, "I am the way and the truth and the life. No one comes to the Father except through me" (John 14:6). If we want to have a saving, joyful, intimate, lasting relationship with God, it comes through Jesus.

In Hebrews 7:26–28, the writer continued to compare the inadequate old priesthood with the perfect priesthood of Christ. While the former priests were weak men (v. 28) and in need of daily sacrifice for their "own sins" (v. 27), Jesus "is holy, blameless, pure, set apart from sinners, exalted above the heavens" (v. 26). He is the "high priest" who "meets our need" (v. 26). While the former priests had "to offer sacrifices day after day . . . He sacrificed . . . once for all when he offered himself" (v. 27). The law appointed the former priests, but God's oath appointed Jesus (v. 28). Not only was Jesus a better priest, but His offering of himself provided a sacrifice far superior to the animals and products of the soil offered on Israel's altars.

Provision of a More-Effective Covenant (Heb. 8:1–7)

In these verses, the writer to the Hebrews asserted that the real **sanctuary** or place of worship, **the true tabernacle**, is in heaven, **set up by the Lord, not by man** (v. 2). It had been **shown** as **the pattern** to Moses **on the mountain**. So the tabernacle Moses built in the wilderness was just **a copy and shadow of what is in heaven** (v. 5). Jesus, our **high priest . . . sat down at the right hand of the throne of the Majesty in heaven** (v. 1), and He serves as the High Priest in the heavenly sanctuary. It is here that He intercedes for us (compare Rom. 8:34; Heb. 7:25).

WORDS FROM WESLEY

Hebrews 8:6

And now he hath obtained a more excellent ministry—His priesthood as much excels theirs, as the promises of the gospel (whereof He is a surety) excel those of the law. These better promises are specified, ver. 10, 11. Those in the law were mostly temporal promises. (ENNT)

The writer went on to say that not only is Jesus' ministry superior to that of the former priesthood, but God has made a new and better covenant with His people. The old agreement between God and Israel was inadequate. If it had not been, **no place would have been sought for another** (8:7). It was common in biblical times for rulers to enter into covenants or agreements with their people. God had entered into covenants in the Old Testament beginning with Noah and continuing with individuals and with His people as a whole. Some covenants were determined entirely by the superior party; some required certain things of both the superior and inferior parties. God's covenant with Israel had stipulated certain things both were to do. That covenant was being replaced. It had failed because the people failed (v. 9). The new covenant was to be based solely on the grace of God. Not only will He do what He has promised to do, but He will *enable* His people to live in obedience to Him.

In 8:8–13, the writer cited Jeremiah 31:31–34, in which the Lord had promised there would be a new covenant. The old one had failed because the people had not been "faithful" (Heb. 8:9). The new covenant was not to be external and materialistic but inward and spiritual. God's law was no longer to be only on stone tablets or scrolls, but "I will put my laws in their minds, and write them on their hearts" (v. 10). There was now to be a personal relationship between God and each person, and no longer would a neighbor or brother be needed to remind them to "know the Lord" because each one would know Him, "from the least of them to the greatest" (v. 11). This "new" covenant rendered "the first one obsolete; and what is obsolete and aging will soon disappear" (v. 13). This new covenant of an inner, spiritual knowledge of and personal relationship with God is what we have in Christ.

DISCUSSION

Many people wrestle with change, but the first Jewish Christians were making a whole-life shift from the old to the new covenant. Hebrews reminds them why the new covenant is superior.

1. Which tribe supplied Israel's priesthood under the law of Moses?

2. Since Jesus belonged to the tribe of Judah, how did He qualify as a high priest?

3. What do you learn about Jesus' priesthood from Hebrews 7:15–17?

4. Compare Hebrews 7:1–3 and Isaiah 9:6–7. How did the priesthood of Melchizedek foreshadow Jesus' priesthood?

5. What does it mean to you personally that Jesus is your High Priest?

6. Why was the old covenant unable to make anything perfect?

7. What significance do you attach to the fact that our High Priest "sat down at the right hand of the throne of the Majesty in heaven" (Heb. 8:1)?

8. Compare Hebrews 8:6–7 and Jeremiah 31:31–34. How is the new covenant better than the old covenant?

9. What are a few ways your life shows that God has written His laws in your heart?

PRAYER

Lord, thank You for the new covenant, purchased by the atoning work of Your Son and our Savior, Jesus. Save us completely, O God, and give us what we need to persevere to the end of our days.

8

THE PRECIOUS BLOOD OF CHRIST

Hebrews 9:11–28

Jesus' death on the cross was the perfect sacrifice.

Jesus spoke these triumphant words—"It is finished!"—from the cross to signify His work of redemption was complete and perfect. Nothing needed to be added to it. The Greek word *tetelestai* literally means, "It stands finished." The word was written on sales transactions to indicate "paid in full." An artist might step back from the canvas, inspect the painting, and exclaim, "Tetelestai," meaning nothing further needed to be done to the work.

This study focuses attention on the perfect sacrifice Jesus offered on the cross. Looking by faith to the cross, we can say with conviction, "Tetelestai!"

COMMENTARY

Why is Jesus' death so important? To answer this question, the writer of Hebrews presented Jesus as our High Priest and His incarnation and death as the ultimate atoning sacrifice for sin. Through this sacrifice God's people can be truly cleansed of sin and have access to God, both now and forever. It was urgent that his readers grasp this reality so they would persevere in faith until the end. He exhorted and urged them with deep pastoral concern, and so it is fitting for this study to refer to the writer of Hebrews as the "pastor."

The pastor demonstrated the full sufficiency of Christ's atoning sacrifice in 8:1—10:18. The theme of sacrifice is by far the greatest, for it is by His sacrifice that the incarnate Son of God opened the way into heaven, the "sanctuary" of God's presence. It is also by this sacrifice that He initiated a new covenant or arrangement of approaching God. Under this covenant there is real forgiveness and true heart cleansing for obedience (10:16–18).

The author stated this theme in relationship to one another. Since Jesus is at God's right hand in the heavenly sanctuary (8:1–2, compare Ps. 110:1), He must have offered a greater sacrifice than those who served in the earthly sanctuary (Heb. 8:3–5). The covenant He established is also superior, as indicated by the prophecy of Jeremiah 31:31–34, quoted in Hebrews 8:8–12. The fact that Jeremiah spoke of a new covenant indicated the old was inadequate (Heb. 8:6–14).

Later, the pastor played this theme in richer harmony by looking back at the Mosaic sanctuary (9:1–10) and covenant (9:16–22). According to 9:1–10, the description of that sanctuary showed that it was woefully inadequate, only a rough draft of what the Son of God would accomplish.

Perfect Sacrifice (Heb. 9:11–15)

There had been no adequate access to God, but **when Christ came as high priest of the good things that are already here** (v. 11), everything changed. The **good things** are forgiveness, heart cleansing, and access to the Father. What did Christ do that was different? He ministered not in a **man-made** tabernacle or temple that was part of **this creation**. He passed through **the greater and more perfect tabernacle** (v. 11) into that heavenly sanctuary of God's presence.

The pastor calls this heavenly sanctuary **the Most Holy Place** (v. 12) by analogy with the inner sanctum of the Mosaic sanctuary, which the high priest could enter only on the Day of Atonement (Lev. 16). Jesus entered the heavenly sanctuary not once every year **but once for all** and forever (Heb. 9:12). On what basis did He enter? Not on the basis of **the blood of goats and calves** like those offered on the Day of Atonement. His was not some animal sacrifice. It was **his own** precious **blood**. He offered himself and **obtained eternal** and effective **redemption** for His people from the guilt and power of sin (v. 12).

WORDS FROM WESLEY

Hebrews 9:12

He it was, who, 'not by the blood of bulls and goats, but by his own blood, entered into the holiest, having obtained eternal redemption for us' (Heb. 9:12). In consequence of this we are accepted, 'through the offering of the body of Christ once for all' (10:10). In all the ancient types and figures, 'without shedding of blood there was no remission;' which was intended to show, there never could be any without the blood of the great Antitype; without that grand propitiatory sacrifice, which (like the figure of it) was to be offered 'without the gate.' (WJW, vol. 9, 492)

Verses 13–14 contrast the **blood of goats and bulls** with **the blood of Christ**. In verse 13, the pastor affirmed that the Old Testament sacrifices provided outward or ritual purification. The **blood of goats and bulls** was sprinkled on the outside and could cleanse only the outside, those who were **ceremonially unclean**. The pastor emphasized the fact that those sacrifices bought outward purity by referring to the ritual use of the **ashes** of the red **heifer** (v. 13). This ritual was only for ceremonial cleansing (Num. 19:1–22).

Since those sacrifices, which did not bring true cleansing and access to God, did bring ceremonial or ritual cleansing, then certainly the **blood of Christ** (Heb. 9:14) must bring much more. First, He offered himself **through the eternal Spirit**. He was the eternal Son of God (1:1–14; 5:5–6) who became a high priest "by the power of an indestructible life" (7:16). Second, He **offered himself unblemished** (9:14). He lived His entire human life in obedience to the Father and thus His self-offering was acceptable. Hebrews 10:5–10 makes the nature of this obedience clear. Since He is the eternal Son of God who lived a completely obedient human life, His self-offering has the power to **cleanse our consciences from acts that lead to death** (9:14). This cleansing takes away the guilt, corruption, and power of sin. The conscience is used here as the equivalent of the heart. By Christ's sacrifice the evil heart of unbelief (3:12) becomes a true heart (10:22). The NIV's **acts that lead to death** is an accurate interpretation of the KJV'S more literal "dead works." Nevertheless, "dead works" is a very expressive phrase. These works encumber the heart and weigh it down, drawing the person to eternal death. The heart is cleansed from being a heart that is attracted to and controlled by the doing of such works. Freedom from this bondage enables the faithful believer to **serve the living God** (9:14). Thus, this cleansing leads to a life of holiness, to a life in which God's laws are written on the heart (see 10:16–18).

WORDS FROM WESLEY

Hebrews 9:14

How much more shall the blood of Christ—The merit of all His sufferings: *who through the eternal Spirit*—The work of redemption being the work of the whole Trinity. Neither is the second person alone concerned even in the amazing condescension that was needful to complete it. The Father delivers up the kingdom to the Son: and the Holy Ghost becomes the gift of the Messiah, being as it were, *sent* according to His good pleasure: *offered himself*—Infinitely more precious than any created victim, and that *without spot to God: purge our conscience*—Our inmost soul, *from dead works*—From all the inward and outward works of the devil, which spring from spiritual death in the soul, and lead to death everlasting: *to serve the living God*—In the life of faith, in perfect love, and spotless holiness! (ENNT)

If Christ's sacrifice makes true atonement for sin and cleanses the believer's heart from its guilt and bondage, then He **is the mediator of a new covenant** (9:15). A new way of approaching God is in effect. This **new covenant** is the means by which God's people can enter the **promised eternal inheritance** (v. 15). Only the eternal Son of God through His obedient human life and atoning death could provide this access. It is through His death that they have been redeemed from those **sins** they **committed under the first covenant** (v. 15), for which that covenant had no adequate remedy.

Jesus' Sacrifice Removes Sin (Heb. 9:16–22)

The Old Testament covenant sacrifices represented the deaths of those who entered into the covenant. Those entering the covenant symbolically pledged their lives if they broke faith.

The word here translated **will** (vv. 16–17) is the same word translated "covenant" in verse 15 and in verses 18–22. It is probably most accurate to translate "covenant" in verses 16–17 as well. Also, the word translated **to prove** in verse 16 does not have that meaning elsewhere, but it can mean "bear" or "bring." Finally, the Greek behind the phrase in verse 17, **when somebody has died**, is "on the basis of deaths."

The **first covenant was . . . put into effect** on the basis of **blood** sacrifices (v. 18). By those sacrifices the Israelites pledged their own deaths for violation of the covenant.

Verse 19 reflects Moses' establishment of the Sinai Covenant in Exodus 24:3–8. First, Moses declared **every commandment of the law to all the people** (Heb. 9:19) so they would adequately understand the covenant before accepting it. Then Moses took the **blood** of the sacrifice and **sprinkled** both **the scroll**, representing God, and **the people**. Exodus actually says that Moses sprinkled the altar and the people. Perhaps the scroll was on the altar. By using the scroll to represent God, the pastor emphasized the necessity of keeping the stipulations of the covenant. Exodus 24 doesn't actually say Moses used **water, scarlet wool and branches of hyssop** (Heb. 9:19), but these were commonly used for purification (Lev. 14:4–9; Num. 19:6–10; Ps. 51:7; John 19:29).

Hebrews 9:20 paraphrases the final words Moses used to establish the covenant in Exodus 24:8: **This is the blood of the covenant, which God has commanded you to keep** (Heb. 9:20). This statement emphasizes the significance of the blood sacrifice and the necessity of keeping what God has commanded. Violation of the covenant invoked one's own death. By the blood of the Old Testament covenant, the people pledged their own deaths for violation. By His sacrifice, however, Christ took that covenant curse on himself and ransomed them from "the sins committed under the first covenant" (v. 15). Our sin stands under the judgment of that covenant law until cleansed by Christ.

The importance of this blood is emphasized by the assertion that Moses sprinkled not only the scroll of the law but also the **tabernacle and everything used in its ceremonies** (v. 21). The sprinkling of blood was pervasive both in establishing the old covenant and in maintaining it. When one lived under the old covenant, almost everything was **cleansed with blood** (v. 22), though a few things were not. Under the old covenant, **without the shedding of blood there is no forgiveness**. The word *remission* in some translations better represents the pastor's thought. More than forgiveness is at stake; it is the remission or the removal of sin. Without blood, there was and is no removal, remission, redemption, or cleansing, and no access to God.

Christ Died Once for All (Heb. 9:23–28)

The high priest purified the Most Holy Place on the Day of Atonement, and these were only **copies of the heavenly** (v. 23) dwelling place of God. If animals were needed to purify the copies, then the original had to be purified with infinitely **better sacrifices**. The sacrifice of Christ brought such purification.

Then the pastor said plainly that the sanctuary Christ entered was not **man-made**; it was not the earthly **copy** (v. 24). **He entered heaven itself**, the eternal dwelling place of God. He had been with God prior to His incarnation, but this time He entered as our high priest, appearing **for us in God's presence** (v. 24). Thus, we are able to draw near to God through Him in order to "receive mercy and find grace to help us in our time of need" (4:16).

In 9:25–28, the pastor wrote more on the sacrificial death of Jesus. The Aaronic high priest went into the Most Holy Place **every year** (v. 25). He entered on the basis of **blood . . . not his own**. Christ, however, did not enter the heavenly sanctuary repeatedly. **He has appeared once for all** (v. 26). According to Psalm 110:1 (see Heb. 1:14), He sat down once for all at God's right hand **at the end of the ages** (9:26), the great turning point of history. He did so to **do away with sin** once and for all. All this could be accomplished only **by the sacrifice of himself** (v. 26).

WORDS FROM WESLEY

Hebrews 9:26

For then he must often have suffered from the foundation of the world—This supposes, 1. That by suffering once, He atoned for all the sins which had been committed from the foundation of the world: 2. That He could not have atoned for them without suffering: *at the consummation of the ages*—The sacrifice of Christ divides the whole age or duration of the world into two parts, and extends its virtue backward and forward, from this middle point wherein they meet, to *abolish* both the guilt and power of *sin*. (ENNT)

By emphasizing that Christ has come once for all and done away with sin, the pastor did not want to deny the second coming and our consequent responsibility before Him at that coming. Every human being must **die once** and **face judgment** (v. 27) at Christ's return (see 12:25–29). Christ has been **sacrificed once to take away the sins of many** and will come a second time **to bring** full and final **salvation** (v. 28) to those who are anticipating

His coming with faith and obedience. **Many** emphasizes the all-inclusiveness of Christ's work. He died only once, but it was totally adequate for the sins of many. He experienced death for all (2:9).

DISCUSSION

Jesus' death on the cross, along with His resurrection, was the pivotal moment of all of history. Hebrews helps its readers come to grips with its significance.

1. How did Israel's high priests enter the Most Holy Place?

2. What evidence do you find in Hebrews 9:11–14 that Jesus' priestly ministry was superior to that of the Old Testament?

3. What evidence do you find in verses 11–14 that Jesus was a superior high priest?

4. How would you answer someone who insists salvation depends on good works, not on Jesus' blood?

5. Based on verse 26, what kind of life did Jesus lead?

6. Why do you agree or disagree that Jesus had to be sinless in order to die for sinners?

7. How did Jesus' once-for-all sacrifice for sin accomplish what the many Old Testament sacrifices could not accomplish?

8. In what sense will Jesus' second coming bring salvation (v. 28)?

9. What will you do for Jesus while you wait for His return?

PRAYER

Lord, thank You for making forgiveness possible through the shedding of Jesus' blood on the cross. Give us the patience, endurance, and wisdom to forgive others as You have forgiven us.

9

WALKING TOGETHER BY FAITH

Hebrews 10:19–39

Our walk of faith is strengthened by fellowship with His people.

Riding a bicycle in heavy traffic is not always easy, but it is best to keep pedaling. Big trouble can befall the cyclist who stops when cars and trucks are behind or beside him or her. Similarly, the Christian life demands that we persevere and encourage one another to do so. We place ourselves in jeopardy if we think we can stop learning, growing, and serving. We must stay the course, spur one another to love and good works, and keep on assembling for fellowship and worship. If we fail to persevere, we run the risk of incurring divine judgment, a consequence far worse than that of a cyclist getting struck by a car or truck.

This study inspires us to keep pedaling!

COMMENTARY

It is easy to become fixated on elements of the letter to the Hebrews that are unknown to us. We do not know the author of the epistle. We don't exactly know when it was written. And we cannot say with absolute assurance who the specific audience was. These open questions could discourage us from believing it is possible to discern a clear and accurate message. But that perspective is a mistake, because the open questions have reasonable, approximate answers and the thrust of the message of Hebrews rings forcefully true.

First, the author was an intellectual, likely from the Jewish priestly class, who had a firm grasp on the content of the Old

Testament and its implications. He was clearly a Christian leader the church revered and trusted. Second, it was written sometime during the second half of the first century A.D. by which time Christianity had spread through the Mediterranean world and had second-generation converts. Third, the probable audience was a group of Jewish Christians who had experienced a measure of persecution from the Roman Empire, likely to experience more. The author wrote to help them better understand God's redemptive work in history culminating in Christ, and he encouraged them to persevere in their faith rather than revert to a mind-set and practices mired in the old covenant, which was only a foreshadowing of the hope found in Jesus Christ.

The overarching theme of the book of Hebrews is that Jesus Christ is the supreme expression of God's redemptive plan in history. The writer said Jesus is the ultimate sacrifice for the sins of human beings and that He is the great High Priest mediating the atoning sacrifice rite on behalf of all humanity. The writer began in chapter 1 by pointing out that in the past God acted decisively in history to make His will known in various ways. He spoke through events, the patriarchs, and the prophets, but the supreme expression of His saving will and work was manifested in Jesus. The writer went on to advance his thesis that Jesus Christ is the ultimate expression of God by saying He is greater than the angels. He continued building his case in chapters 3–4 by declaring that Jesus is greater than Moses—the most revered of all past Hebrew luminaries. In chapters 4–7, the writer made it clear that Jesus is also superior to the whole Aaronic priesthood. The ritualistic work of the priests appeased God through the bloody, tedious, and cumbersome sacrificial system, but Christ is the one high priest who supersedes the whole line of Aaronic priests by presiding over the once-and-for-all atonement.

The message of the letter then builds to a climax in chapters 8–10, where the writer declared that Jesus Christ is the one and only sacrifice that was possible and needed for the salvation of all persons. The crescendo of the climax comes in Hebrews 9:14: "How much more, then, will the blood of Christ, who through the eternal Spirit offered himself unblemished to God, cleanse our consciences from acts that lead to death, so that we may serve the living God!"

Once the writer established that Christ is the supreme, efficacious sacrifice to provide salvation, his attention turned to the practical implications of Christ's redemptive work for believers.

Christocentric Implications and Exhortations (Heb. 10:19–25)

Therefore (v. 19) indicates a pivot in the thematic thrust of the author's message. Since Christ's sacrifice made obsolete the old sacrificial system, there are practical implications for believers. The endearing term **brothers** suggests that the author wrote with a familial tenderness and pleading. While Hebrews is a scholarly theological treatise, it was written with warm pastoral sentiment. The writer appealed to his readers to embrace these ideas and let them have full effect in their lives.

We have confidence to enter the Most Holy Place by the blood of Jesus (v. 19). In observance of the old covenant directives, the high priest entered the Most Holy Place of the tabernacle once a year, never more often, and presented the blood of a bull and goat in atonement for the sins of God's people over the previous year (see Lev. 16). The high priest approached this ritual with trepidation and fastidious attention to detail. He did not want to violate any element of the sacrificial regulations for fear of incurring the wrath of God. In contrast to the climate of the old sacrificial rite is the climate of approaching God because of Jesus' sacrifice. A Christian can step into God's presence with authorization, certainty, and assurance. **A new and living way opened for us** (Heb. 10:20). Under the old covenant only the high priest had direct access to God for atonement of sins, but now all barriers created by sin have been destroyed and Christ is the means by which anyone can have direct access to God. The motif of confidence is one that was clearly on the writer's mind throughout the letter (see 3:14; 4:16; 6:9; 10:22; 10:35). To the writer, confidence in approaching God comes from a clear conscience, and a clear conscience is made possible by accepting the provision of forgiveness of sins through Christ's sacrifice. No longer does a person have to be haunted by the guilt of sins committed (see 9:14; 10:22; 13:18). In this notion of confidence, we see the author's pastoral impulse—he did not want anyone to miss the relief and exhilaration of a clear conscience and the consequent confidence that comes in approaching God.

WORDS FROM WESLEY

Hebrews 10:20

By a living way—The way of faith, whereby we live indeed: *Which he hath consecrated*—Prepared, dedicated, and established, *for us, through the veil*—That is, *his flesh*—As by rending the veil in the temple, the holy of holies became visible and accessible, so by wounding the body of Christ, the God of heaven was manifested, and the way to heaven opened. (ENNT)

Since believers can have confidence through the saving work of Christ, how should they behave? The writer gave a flurry of exhortations to answer that question. First, **let us hold unswervingly to the hope we profess** (10:23). The writer gave numerous exhortations to persevere and hang on for dear life to our beliefs in Christ. Note these expressions: "Fix your thoughts on Jesus" (3:1); "We have come to share in Christ if we hold firmly till the end" (3:14); "Let us hold firmly to the faith we profess" (4:14); "Let us run with perseverance" (12:1). The intensity and frequency of these "hold on" exhortations suggests that the writer was deeply concerned that these Christians were drifting in their faith and that their defection from the Christian faith was a distinct possibility. Second, **Let us consider how we may spur one another on toward love and good deeds** (10:24). To be a Christian is to look like Christ in our conduct. Christians must consciously work to enact the ethos of Christ as taught and exemplified in the Gospels. A Christian who has been freed from guilt can rest and relax in God's grace, but he or she must exert great moral effort to be like Christ. We can never *earn* our salvation, but Christians should make every *effort* to live in accordance with their salvation. They should incite and stimulate each other to do good works. Third, **Let us not give up meeting together** (v. 25). A manifestation of the spiritual drift of some of the Christians mentioned in 2:1 was their failure to gather together in worship and fellowship. The tone of this strongly worded exhortation suggests the importance of gathering with other believers. Fourth, **Let us encourage one another—and all the more as you see the Day approaching** (10:25). Believers should remind each other of the fundamentals of Christian faith and practice in anticipation of the day when Christ will come a second time.

WORDS FROM WESLEY

Hebrews 10:25

Not forsaking the assembling ourselves—In public or private worship, *as the manner of some is*—Either through fear of persecution, or from a vain imagination that they were above external ordinances: *but exhorting one another*—To faith, love, and good works; *and so much the more, as ye see the day approaching*—The great day is ever in your eye. (ENNT)

When these "let us" exhortations are taken together, they emphasize that Christians do not exist as isolated spiritual beings practicing an individualized faith. Instead each Christian belongs to every other Christian, and each one has the responsibility to be sensitive and submissive to his or her brothers and sisters, and is also charged with the task of monitoring and caring for the welfare of his or her brothers and sisters.

A Chilling Warning (Heb. 10:26–31)

If we deliberately keep on sinning after we have received the knowledge of the truth, no sacrifice for sins is left, but only a fearful expectation of judgment and of raging fire (vv. 26–27). The writer delivered his message of Christ's sacrifice with pathos, tenderness, and pastoral urging. He pled with readers to take full advantage of God's redemptive bounty made possible by Christ's death on the cross. He reiterated that the opportunities to be experienced through Christ are unprecedented and incomparable. But on a few occasions in the text the writer conveyed a stern warning. This message is the flipside of the coin of the good news. It is the possibility of a tragic outcome. Essentially the writer said that since God's grace expressed in Christ's redemptive work is so grand, to discard it, ignore it, or harden our hearts against it would bring catastrophic consequences. And so the book of Hebrews contains urgings and warnings not to cast away the only means whereby a person can be saved; otherwise a harsh judgment is inevitable. In verse 28, the writer alluded to a law from the book of Deuteronomy. He reminded the reader that just as worshiping other gods in the Hebrew community brought upon one the penalty of death, so anyone rejecting Christ's sacrifice would experience God's wrath (see Deut. 17:2–7). Since Christ is the only means of salvation, to reject Him would be folly. The repeated warnings of the writer to these drifting believers not to "harden your hearts" (3:8; 4:7) and the reminders that if they reject Christ their doom was sealed (6:4–7; 10:26) were designed to help these believers appreciate the gravity of what was at stake.

WORDS FROM WESLEY

Hebrews 10:28

Such a sense of sin . . . together with a full conviction, such as no words can express, that of Christ only cometh our salvation, and an earnest desire of that salvation, must precede a living faith, a trust in Him, who "for us paid our ransom by his death, and fulfilled the law in his life." This faith then, whereby we are born of God, is "not only a belief of all the articles of our faith, but also a true confidence of the mercy of God, through our Lord Jesus Christ." (WJW, vol. 5, 214)

It would be unwise to take these warning texts and stitch together a doctrine of an unpardonable sin. The writer of Hebrews did not appear to build a case that a certain sin is so egregious that it merits automatic damnation. The only sin that is unpardonable is an unconfessed sin hidden away in a hardened heart (see Matt. 12:32). Any sin can be immediately cleansed away if it is confessed and Christ's sacrifice is embraced for that sin (see 1 John 1:9). Such is the expanse of God's grace expressed in Christ. Still, the writer of Hebrews pointed out the alarming and devastating consequences for rejecting Christ's sacrifice for sin.

A Plea to Persevere (Heb. 10:32–39)

In this section, the writer revisited a frequently mentioned motif—perseverance (Heb. 12:1ff.). He called these Christians to hold on to their confidence in Christ's redemptive work and not to acquiesce to any moments of doubt or to quit because of adversity. With the words **stood side by side** (10:33), the writer emphasized the mutuality and communal nature in their past experience of the Christian faith. He insisted that if Christians are to persevere in their faith it will be in part through the encouragement and loyalty of brothers and sisters in Christ. **You sympathized with those in prison and joyfully accepted the confiscation of your property** (v. 34). The writer harkened back to trials these Christians experienced in the past to prepare them for additional assaults. It is likely that the Roman Empire was starting (or restarting) a campaign of terror against these Christians (perhaps under the reign of Nero ca. A.D. 64 or Domitian ca. A.D. 85). **So do not throw away your confidence; it will be richly rewarded** (v. 35). In verse 35, we start to see the writer's transition to his next theme. The foundation of perseverance is confidence and faith in God.

DISCUSSION

Too often we think of Christianity primarily as a personal and individual faith. But Christ-followers are called into community, and community helps us persevere in faith.

1. What personal privileges do you find in Hebrews 10:19–20?

2. What personal obligations do you find in verses 22–25?

3. How has a fellow Christian encouraged you recently? How have you encouraged a fellow Christian recently?

4. How would you describe the consequences of rejecting Christ's sacrifice (vv. 26–31)?

5. Why do you agree or disagree that God's justice and wrath are seldom taught in books and sermons?

6. What do see as the greatest threats to faith?

7. How had the Hebrews demonstrated persevering faith in the past (vv. 32–34)?

8. What are a few past experiences that have bolstered your present confidence in the Lord?

9. Does the hope of being rewarded for doing God's will help you persevere? If so, how?

PRAYER

Lord, give us clean hearts and spotless consciences as we confess our sins to You, blaming no one but ourselves for what we have chosen. Thank You for the full assurance that faith brings.

10

FAITH THAT MOVES GOD

Hebrews 11:1–16

Run the race of faith with perseverance.

The United States is home to several sports halls of fame. For example, Canton, Ohio, is the site of the Pro Football Hall of Fame. Cooperstown, New York, hosts the National Baseball Hall of Fame, and Springfield, Massachusetts, is home to the Basketball Hall of Fame. Sports fans readily recognize most of the names inscribed in those halls.

Hebrews 11 has been called the Hall of Faith chapter of the Bible. Most of the names that appear there are readily recognized, but many other people are unnamed. It is an impressive roster of men and women of faith who are worthy of our emulation.

This study stimulates us to have faith in God as we seek to honor and serve Him.

COMMENTARY

Hebrews 10 ends with a strong emphasis on faith. Verse 38 quotes from Habakkuk 2:3–4, one of the greatest Old Testament statements on faith: "My righteous one will live by faith." And Hebrews 10:39 declares, "We are not of those who shrink back and are destroyed, but of those who believe and are saved." These verses provide the perfect springboard from which to launch the writer's discourse on faith in chapter 11.

Chapter 11 is the great "faith chapter" of the Bible. The writer had been encouraging his readers in many ways throughout the epistle not to doubt, but to believe. In 11:1–3, he explained the significance of faith. Beginning in verse 4, he called the roll of those in faith's hall of fame—painting word portraits of them in a gallery of the heroes of faith.

WORDS FROM WESLEY

Hebrews 11:1

Now faith is the subsistence of things hoped for, the evidence or *conviction of things not seen—Things hoped for* are not so extensive as *things not seen*. The former are only things future, and joyful to us; the latter are either future, past, or present, and those either good or evil, whether to us or others. *The subsistence of things hoped for*—Giving a kind of present subsistence to the good things which God has promised; the divine, supernatural evidence exhibited to, the conviction hereby produced in a believer, *of things not seen*—Whether past, future, or spiritual; particularly of God, and the things of God. (ENNT)

The Significance of Faith (Heb. 11:1–3)

The writer to the Hebrews began his treatise of faith by helping his readers understand the importance of faith—its practical effect in the life of the believer. **Faith is being sure of what we hope for** (v. 1). The original word for **being sure of** had three possible meanings, all of which have some application here: (1) "Substance" or the reality that underlies what we see, or in this case, what we hope for; (2) "foundation" or that which "stands under," that which gives a basis to hopes that would otherwise be little more than wistful desires; and (3) "assurance," a word that was commonly used in business documents as the basis or guarantee of transactions. The writer went on to say, **Faith is being . . . certain of what we do not see** (v. 1). The word for **certain** here is a strong word that means "proof" or "conviction." It was frequently used of putting something to a test, demonstrating or proving that it is so. It is being convinced of the truth of that which is not seen. So faith is not some flight of fancy, being lost in imagination. It brings with it both a guarantee and a conviction.

WORDS FROM WESLEY

Hebrews 11:1

In particular, faith is an evidence to me of the existence of that unseen thing. . . . I know by faith that, above all these, is the Lord Jehovah; He that is, that was, and that is to come; that is God from everlasting, and world without end; He that filleth heaven and earth; He that is infinite in power, in wisdom, in justice, in mercy, and holiness; He that created all things, visible and invisible, by the breath of His mouth, and still upholds them all, preserves them in being, "by the word of his power;" and that governs all things that are in heaven above, in earth beneath, and under the earth. By faith I know, "there are Three that bear record in heaven, the Father, the Word, and the Holy Spirit, and that these Three are One"; that the Word, God the Son, "was made flesh," lived and died for our salvation, rose again, ascended into heaven, and now sitteth on the right hand of the Father. By faith I know that the Holy Spirit is the giver of all spiritual life; of righteousness, peace, and joy in the Holy Ghost; of holiness and happiness, by the restoration of that image of God wherein we are created. Of all these things, faith is the evidence, the sole evidence, to the children of men. (WJW, vol. 7, 232–233)

This is what the ancients were commended for (v. 2) **Ancients** refers to the ancestors of the Jewish nation, whose stories were told in the Old Testament. The writer to the Hebrews had built a powerful argument to demonstrate that Christ is superior to all other religious leaders, and His new covenant is superior to the old. Then he turned to the practical application of all he had said and called for his readers to be "of those who believe and are saved" (10:39), and he prepared to show it was by faith that the ancients had pleased God. Faith is not some new substitute for the old covenant and the law. Rather, it was the basis on which those were initiated. He bound the Jewish Christians of the New Testament era with their past, and also bound us with all who have gone before. He went on to show in the rest of the chapter the significance of faith in the history of God's dealing with His people, setting it forth in the individual and cumulative stories of those who made a difference by believing God.

The writer began at the beginning. He cited belief about the origin of our universe as one of the practical ways in which faith's significance is demonstrated. **By faith we understand that the universe was formed at God's command, so that what is seen was not made out of what was visible** (11:3). This is a clear reference to the story of Genesis 1. No human was on hand to observe the early stages of creation. We cannot know about it on the basis of physical sense or human reason. So the only way we can know about it is by divine revelation. God told us about it in His Word, and by faith we can be as sure and certain of it as any of the things we know through sight or touch.

The Witnesses to Faith (Heb. 11:4–16)

Our study features five heroes of faith described in Hebrews 11:4–16.

The story in Genesis 4 about Cain and Abel does not speak of faith as a factor in Abel's successful worship. That account has led some to suppose Abel's sacrifice was preferable because it involved the shedding of the sacrificial animal's blood. Cain brought of the fruits of the soil. However, the Old Testament sacrificial system included not only animal sacrifices, but sacrifices of grain, wine, olive oil, and incense as well (see Ex. 29:40; Num. 7:13–14). So both Cain and Abel had brought what they had to offer. It was not the *offering* that made the difference, but the *offerer*. **By faith Abel offered God a better sacrifice than Cain did** (Heb. 11:4). Faith made the difference. We are not told what prompted Abel's faith. Perhaps he had heard of God's promise of a future deliverer made to Eve in Genesis 3:15. Or perhaps it was God's sacrifice of animals to make skin garments for Adam and Eve in 3:21. Cain apparently offered as a mere formality. Faith is essential for worship.

Enoch was one who **by faith . . . was taken from this life, so that he did not experience death** (Heb. 11:5). Like Moses, whose body God hid, Enoch **could not be found**, but for him it was **because God had taken him away** (v. 5; compare Gen. 5:24; Deut. 34:1–8). **Before he was taken, he was commended as one who pleased God** (Heb. 11:5). **Commended** is the same word in verse 2, and **commended** and **spoke well of** in verse 4. It was faith that enabled Enoch to please God. He lived such a holy life that God took him heavenward about five hundred years before others in his age were dying.

WORDS FROM WESLEY

Hebrews 11:6

And, indeed, unless the servants of God halt by the way, they will receive the adoption of sons. They will receive the *faith* of the children of God, by His *revealing* His only begotten Son in their hearts. Thus, the faith of a child is, properly and directly, a divine conviction, whereby every child of God is enabled to testify, "The life that I now live, I live by faith in the Son of God, who loved me, and gave himself for me." And whosoever hath this, the Spirit of God witnesseth with his spirit, that he is a child of God. So the apostle writes to the Galatians: "Ye are the sons of God by faith. And because ye are sons, God bath sent forth the Spirit of his Son into your hearts, crying, Abba, Father;" that is, giving you a childlike confidence in Him, together with a kind affection toward Him. (WJW, vol. 7, 199)

In 11:6, the writer followed up on the reference to Enoch's pleasing God by saying that **without faith it is impossible to please God**. Two acts of faith are required: **believe that** God **exists and that he rewards those who earnestly seek him** (v. 6).

No one could come **to him** if they did not believe in His existence. But more is required. The one coming to God must believe that God relates to humans, to the point of giving rewards. To believe God exists and made all things falls short if we think of God as someone detached from His creation, unavailable to us. Faith is the key to a better understanding and a real relationship.

Noah (v. 7) is next on the roll of faith's heroes. His **faith** caused him to take it seriously when he was **warned about things not yet seen**. Others no doubt scoffed at him for building an ark on dry land. But **in holy fear** he was enabled **to save his family. By his faith he condemned the world and became heir of the righteousness that comes by faith** (v. 7).

Abraham (v. 8) appears next. In Romans 4:11, Paul called him "the father of all who believe," not only of the Jews, but also of the Christians. So he is our spiritual father as well. Three demonstrations of his outstanding faith are mentioned in Hebrews 11, two in this study (vv. 8–10, 11–12), plus another later in the chapter (vv. 17–19). The first one had to do with his response to God's call to leave the cultured city life he had always known in Mesopotamia. He was **to go to a place he would later receive as his inheritance**. He **obeyed and went, even though he did not know where he was going** (v. 8). There, **he**, his son, and his grandson **lived** not inside city walls, but **in tents** (v. 9). This was because **he was looking forward**, beyond the physical Promised Land, **to the city with foundations, whose architect and builder is God** (v. 10).

In the second demonstration of faith, **Abraham** shares attention with **Sarah** (v. 11). **He was past age** and she **was barren**. But they had a son **by faith**. It was because Abraham **considered him faithful who had made the promise** (v. 11). Even though he was **as good as dead** (v. 12), he had **descendants as numerous as the stars in the sky and as countless as the sand on the seashore** (v. 12).

Then the writer paused in his storytelling to state something of a summary about the persons thus far. They all **were still living by faith when they died. They did not receive the things promised; they only saw them and welcomed them from a distance** (v. 13). They were **aliens and strangers on** this **earth** (v. 13). **They** were **looking for a country of their own . . . a better country—a heavenly one. . . . For God . . . has prepared a city for them** (vv. 14, 16). Only tents while here, but a city yet to come. The book of Revelation had probably not yet been written, but our thoughts go immediately to the new Jerusalem of Revelation 21:1–7.

WORDS FROM WESLEY

Hebrews 11:16

But they desire a better country, that is, an heavenly—This is a full, convincing proof, that the patriarchs had a revelation and a promise of eternal glory in heaven. (ENNT)

The writer to the Hebrews renewed the calling of the roll in 11:17 with the story about Abraham's near offering of Isaac as a burnt offering to the Lord. He then proceeded through the Old Testament and possibly the intertestamental period, when the Maccabees and others lived by faith. And he said in 11:39–40, that none of these heroes "received what had been promised [because] God had planned something better for us so that only together with us would they be made perfect" or complete. All of us together will inherit the promises God began to give so long ago.

DISCUSSION

Hebrews 11 is not so much about heroes as it is about faith. And faith is a virtue that anyone can acquire as the Holy Spirit works in our hearts to bring about transformation.

1. Read Hebrews 11:1, and then define faith in your own words. How accurate is your definition in light of this verse?

2. Why do you agree or disagree that it takes a belief that is not so different from faith to accept a scientific theory such as evolution?

3. Read Hebrews 11:4–10. Which example of faith do you consider most astonishing? Why?

4. Enoch "was commended as one who pleased God" (v. 5). How would you describe the life of faith that pleases God?

5. How might having faith make you feel like an alien and stranger on the earth?

6. Read Hebrews 12:1. Do you think departed believers watch us? Why or why not?

7. What may distract you from running the Christian race with perseverance and with your eyes fixed on Jesus? How will you avoid those distractions?

PRAYER

Lord, encourage us with the examples of faith of the saints of old, and the faithful ones today. Thank You for saving faith, which spurs us on to acts of service and righteousness.

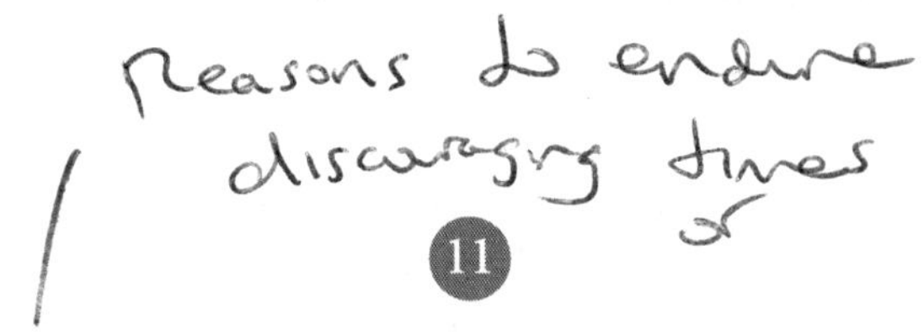

11

NEW LIFE CHANGES EVERYTHING

Hebrews 12:14–29

God has promised new life that requires us to live it.

A mother asked her five-year-old son what he was drawing. "I'm drawing a picture of God," he replied.

"But no one knows what God looks like," Mom said.

The boy glanced at his mother. "They will when I finish this picture."

Many adults, too, draw their own pictures of God, depicting Him to be what they want Him to be. However, their representations of Him often contrast with the biblical portrayal of God as not only loving, merciful, and forgiving, but also holy, righteous, and just. Furthermore, He has summoned His children to live righteously and pursue holiness.

This study will encourage us to walk daily in true holiness.

COMMENTARY

A quick review of Hebrews' thematic content will help us understand our present study passage in chapter 12.

The book can easily be broken down into thematic patterns with appropriate asides and additional arguments from Jewish cultural logic and Scripture. God spoke through His Son (1:1); this is altogether better than through angels (1:4) or even through Moses (3:3). Jesus is a better high priest (4:14), even better than Melchizedek (6:20). Jesus provides a better rest (3:11), better promises (4:1), a better covenant (7:22), a better priesthood (7:26), a better tabernacle (9:11), and a better sacrifice (9:23).

Consequently this brings a better, more complete salvation (2:3; 5:9; 10:2). Therefore, we who participate in this astounding salvation should be better people (10:19), not backsliders (10:26), full of faith (11:1), full of endurance (12:1), and full of steadfast love (13:1).

Chapter 11 of Hebrews is the faith chapter. It gives a listing of men and women of faith and in some instances the cost of their faith to their personal well-being. Part of the emphasis is that the "payoff" for faith is not necessarily always physical or imminent. The last two verses of chapter 11 spell that out specifically. The theme of spiritual recompense occurs again at the end of chapter 12.

Chapter 12 begins with a "therefore," indicating progression of the argument. There are two concepts here. One is that expressed above, that recompense is not always physical and imminent. The second is that sometimes physical recompense is for another generation. This applies to us, and it applies by implication to generations that will follow us. We stand on both sides of this equation. So the evangelist writer moved to the bottom line and hit the ground running in 12:1–3.

While "discipline" can mean punishment, and punishment is indicated in 12:6, the major emphasis in 12:4–11 is the kind of discipline that the motivated runner would put him- or herself under in order to run the race. The discipline of a loving father is not done to inflict misery, but to ingrain protective and positive boundaries so that goals might be reached. The illustration has direct implications in that "God disciplines us for our good, that we may share in his holiness" (12:10). These concepts all lead to the section we want to study with another "therefore" (12:12). Following are some specifics of the discipline regimen.

Holy People Try Harder (Heb. 12:14–17)

In 12:14–28, the writer focused on living a better life. He began with the simple command to **make every effort to live in peace**

with all men (v. 14). The Christian life cannot be lived on cruise control. The concept of making every effort is a cognitive, persistent pursuit. It's a "put your back into it" kind of pursuit. A mistaken idea of peace in the Old Testament was that it was something God would do without our help. This led, for instance, to the lifestyle pictured in Judges 17:6: "Everyone did as he saw fit." The presence of the carnal nature makes living in peace with others a difficult task indeed. However, the Christlike person has the Holy Spirit's help in pursuing peace.

The statement **without holiness no one will see the Lord** (Heb. 12:14) is sometimes quoted out of context. Holiness can be both progressive and a finished work of heart purity. The passage here is a part of the **make every effort** concept. It is progressive. Verse 14 in the KJV appears to be closer in some ways to the Greek text than the NIV. It says, "Follow peace with all men and holiness, with out which no man shall see the Lord." The thing that will keep us from seeing the Lord is failing to follow holiness.

Entire sanctification is not static. There is growth after the first moment (crisis) of entire sanctification. Holiness, whether before entire sanctification or following the cleansing of the sinful nature, is never static. Some have used the logic that if a person has not been entirely sanctified, then he or she can legitimately be impure with immunity, that sin is unimportant in God's eyes at certain stages of the Christian life. Not true. This passage means that from the very first spiritual breath of new birth, God expects us to be pursuers of holiness. A part of that holiness requires making every effort and includes progression. Immaturity is not an excuse for being unholy; God requires the pursuit of holiness, or we will never see Him. The whole concept is based in this better salvation provided by Christ. There are two foundational keys that relate to entire sanctification in this passage. The first is the holiness that begins at salvation, or, as

John Wesley called it, "initial sanctification." The second is the grace of God mentioned in verse 15: **See to it that no one misses the grace of God.**

WORDS FROM WESLEY

Hebrews 12:15

And do we not feel other tempers, which are as contrary to the love of our neighbour as these are to the love of God? The love of our neighbour "thinketh no evil." Do not we find anything of the kind? Do we never find any *jealousies*, any *evil surmisings*, any groundless or unreasonable suspicions? He that is clear in these respects, let him cast the first stone at his neighbour. Who does not sometimes feel other tempers or inward motions, which he knows are contrary to brotherly love? If nothing of *malice, hatred*, or *bitterness*, is there no touch of *envy;* particularly toward those who enjoy some real or supposed good, which we desire but cannot attain? Do we never find any degree of *resentment*, when we are injured or affronted; especially by those whom we peculiarly loved, and whom we had most laboured to help or oblige? Does injustice or ingratitude never excite in us any desire of *revenge*? any desire of returning evil for evil, instead of "overcoming evil with good?" This also shows, how much is still in our heart, which is contrary to the love of our neighbour. (WJW, vol. 5, 160)

The definition of grace as being the "unmerited favor of God" is a truth that is often quoted. But the **make every effort** (v. 14) portion of grace is sometimes overlooked or misrepresented. In this passage, it is expressed by, **See to it that no one misses** (v. 15). Grace is unmerited favor, but God doesn't shove it down our throats. He offers it to us. The implication is that grace can be missed.

The Bible in story, explicit command, and implication shows us that God likes to work cooperatively with us. God is sovereign, and, if He wants, He can send a flood to wipe out the world, harden Pharaoh's heart, or in the end destroy the world. If He wants to, He can. But God is so big that He can also offer unmerited favor to you and actually allow you to make a choice without altering Him or His ultimate plan no matter how you choose. Your response to His grace will have an effect on you. Actually, your response to God's grace may affect others as well. If the **bitter root grows up**, it will **cause trouble and defile many** (v. 15).

WORDS FROM WESLEY

Hebrews 12:17

He was rejected—He could not obtain it: *for he found no place of repentance*—There was no room for any such repentance, as would regain what he had lost, *though he sought it*—The blessing of *the birthright, diligently with tears*—He sought too late. Let us use the present time! (ENNT)

A pastor asked John Wesley how often he should preach on entire sanctification and Wesley's response was "scarcely at all." His whole approach was to teach about God's grace and responding always positively to God's grace. The natural result would lead to the experience of holiness of heart. He said, "Teach free grace not free will." He taught that sin is "a willful transgression against the known law of God." The exact opposite of that would be faith: willful acceptance and obedience to the known law of God. The space between sin and faith is grace, the unmerited favor of God.

We don't deserve it, but we must respond to it one way or the other and everyone does. The point the Hebrews writer was making is that God's grace is overwhelming. Now what are you going to do? The sin aspect mentioned in verses 16–17 is not a little glitch; he mentioned **sexual** immorality and being **godless.** Those things would fit Wesley's sin definition, and the consequence is a loss of inheritance. **See to it that no one misses the**

grace of God (v. 15). Missing the grace misses the mark; it misses the narrow path and misses the inheritance. Responding to grace positively is faith. Responding to grace negatively is sin. Persistent positive response to grace is the path of holiness. That is why without the pursuit of holiness we will never see the Lord.

Who Is the God You Serve? (Heb. 12:18–24)

In the Old Testament, God is often portrayed as a transcendent Being of power and wrath. This is depicted in verses 18–21. He is the God on the mountain **burning with fire . . . darkness, gloom and storm** and **trumpet blast** (vv. 18–19). And the whole thing was so overwhelming and terrifying that even poor old **Moses said, "I am trembling with fear"** (v. 21). Verse 22 begins with the word **but**, which indicates a contrast. If it was set to music, verses 18–21 could be the "March of the Charioteers" from *Ben Hur* with kettle drums and cymbals. The contrast in verses 22–24 might be music taken from the *Sound of Music* with lightness and joy on the mountaintop to the accompaniment of stringed instruments. One depicts transcendence; the other depicts immanence. One is the God away and aloof, powerful and fearful. The other depicts the God with us—Immanuel, near us, who knows us by name and gives to us **a better word** (v. 24).

Remember that this was being offered to a Jewish audience. In these two sections (vv. 18–21 as contrasted to vv. 22–23), the writer of Hebrews pulled in the picture of everything he'd previously written in the book and, as a true evangelist, demanded a cognitive response to grace.

WORDS FROM WESLEY

Hebrews 12:22

But ye—Who believe in Christ, *are come*—The apostle does not here speak of their coming to the church militant, but of that glorious privilege of New Testament believers, their communion with the church triumphant. But this is far more apparent to the eyes of celestial spirits than to ours which are yet veiled. St. Paul here shows an excellent knowledge of the heavenly economy, worthy of him who had been caught up into the third heaven, *to mount Sion*—A spiritual mountain, *to the city of the living God, the heavenly Jerusalem*—All these glorious titles belong to the New Testament church, *and to an innumerable company*—Including all that are afterward mentioned. (ENNT)

Cooperating with God (Heb. 12:25–29)

As a true evangelist, the writer also felt compelled to give a warning, just as he did in chapter 10. **See to it that you do not refuse him who speaks** (12:25). The theological term for cooperating with God is *synergism*. The work of salvation was God's work alone, but He offers it to us. We, by an act of faith, must reach out and take hold of this great salvation. That is synergism. God, in His infinite goodness, speaks to us, offers His grace to us, but we must listen. We must respond. That is synergism. "See to it that no one misses the grace of God" (12:15); **See to it the you do not refuse him who speaks** (v. 25). What a concept! The sovereign God who created the universe by a word, this God of transcendent might, can offer us His grace and speak His word to us, and we can miss the grace and refuse Him. We can **turn away from him** (v. 25). Indeed, "How shall we escape if we ignore such a great salvation?" (2:3).

WORDS FROM WESLEY

Hebrews 12:25

Now, then, "strive to enter in at the strait gate," being penetrated with the deepest sense of the inexpressible danger your soul is in, so long as you are in a broad way—so long as you are void of poverty of spirit, and all that inward religion, which the many, the rich, the wise, account madness. "Strive to enter in"; being pierced with sorrow and shame for having so long run on with the unthinking crowd, utterly neglecting, if not despising, that "holiness without which no man can see the Lord." Strive, as in an agony of holy fear, lest "a promise being made you of entering into his rest," even that "rest which remaineth for the people of God," you should nevertheless "come short of it." (WJW, vol. 5, 412)

The writer's purpose was not to scare his readers; his purpose was to bring them to the logical conclusion. The logic of verses 26–27 might seem a little shaky in our culture, but the point is solidly clear. There is a metaphysical and physical world. One is shaky ground; the other cannot be shaken. Our greatest concern should be the metaphysical—the spiritual world; it alone is the real deal. **Therefore, since we are receiving a kingdom that cannot be shaken, let us be thankful, and so worship God acceptably with reverence and awe, for our "God is a consuming fire"** (vv. 28–29).

DISCUSSION

Though God transforms us, spiritual transformation is not about simply waiting for Him to do the work. It requires effort on our part as well. Hebrews shows the way.

1. Why is it often hard to live in peace with others, as instructed in Hebrews 12:14?

2. Why do you agree or disagree that it takes effort to lead a holy life?

3. Why do you agree or disagree that sexual immorality among believers is increasing? What factors do you think contribute to sexual immorality?

4. Why is bitterness such a destructive quality?

5. Esau is called "godless" in verse 16. What was his sin, and how can a believer today avoid committing this sin?

6. What indications of God's holiness do you see in verses 18–21?

7. Read verses 22–28. What characteristics of the spiritual kingdom make it far superior to the present world?

8. What thoughts and emotions are awakened in you as you contemplate the fact that "God is a consuming fire" (v. 29)?

PRAYER

Lord, give us the courage to face those issues that remain unresolved. Give us grace, patience, and listening ears as we attempt to resolve any conflicts.

12

HOLY ACTIONS FOLLOW HOLY MOTIVES

Hebrews 13:1–21

We are expected and equipped by the Spirit to live holy lives.

Someone quipped, "I can't believe the things that go on in my kid's school: drugs, sex, shootings, stabbings, stealing. At least we have managed to keep prayer out of the classroom." Modern culture is drowning in sin while refusing to call on God for help.

Certainly the culture at its worst needs the church at its best. As Hebrews 13 points out, Christians ought to maintain high standards of love, purity, and holiness in every area of life. Our hearts and minds ought to be pure; our homes ought to be hospitable; and our churches ought to be peaceful.

This study inspires us to let our light shine in many directions.

COMMENTARY

While the style of Hebrews 13 is different from the rest of the book, there is still progression of thought. The word *therefore* in 12:28 ties in chapter 13 to the earlier chapters. This transition could be loosely translated: "If it has been proven in the previous chapters that Jesus brings us a better, more complete way of salvation and holiness, a better understanding of the kingdom of God, and a better understanding of who God is, what are some specifics of practical Christian life and faith?" The answer is chapter 13.

Brotherly Love (Heb. 13:1)

The first practical aspect of Christian life is to **keep on loving each other as brothers** (v. 1). This was an admonition Jesus gave His disciples in John 13:34–35: "A new command I give you: Love one another. As I have loved you, so you must love one another. By this all men will know that you are my disciples, if you love one another" (compare also 1 Pet. 1:22).

The great majority of people in the world outside the church have no interest in our theological debates or religious arguments. The razor-sharp arguments that the Hebrew writer so aptly laid out in the rest of the book leave the majority of the unsaved world of his day, and ours, cold, bored, and uninterested. There is only one argument the church has that attracts the world, and that is love. When a church body falls apart because of infighting and carnal recrimination, the church not only loses its vision, but also its mission. All that precedes and all that follows in the book of Hebrews rests on this point.

Compassion (Heb. 13:2–3)

Among the BaTonga people of Zambia, there is a proverb that says, "The stranger's seat is for sitting and his mouth is for eating." Hebrews says to **entertain strangers** (v. 2). Entertaining strangers includes compassion for those we don't know, who live far away, but surely it also means those who are near at hand. Compassion for tsunami victims whom we don't know and have never met is a part of entertaining strangers too. Jo Anne Lyon, founder of World Hope International, told of going to view the devastation of Sierra Leone following the civil war there. A journalist from one of the major US newspapers traveled with her. The journalist kept asking, "What are you going to do about this?" Jo Anne's reaction was defensive; what could she do? She had no money, no foundations, no means. Surely this wasn't her responsibility—or was it?

> WORDS FROM WESLEY
>
> *Hebrews 13:2*
>
> *Some*—Abraham and Lot, *have entertained angels unawares*—So may an unknown guest, even now, be of more worth than he appears, and may have angels attending him, though unseen. (ENNT)

While love must start at home, it must go beyond home if it is true. Christian compassion reaches out to **those in prison** and to **those who are mistreated** and **suffering** (v. 3) whether across the street, state, nation, or world.

Sexual Purity (Heb. 13:4)

Married Sex Is Good. In verse 4, the writer gave three aspects of sexual purity that are Christian standards. The first is a positive statement about sex within the marriage relationship: **Marriage should be honored by all, and the marriage bed kept pure.** Throughout church history there have been elements of the Christian community who have rejected all sex, even in marriage. Most notable was the Shaker community in nineteenth and early twentieth centuries. Their misunderstanding of Scripture made biological growth of the community impossible and conversion to the community unattractive, so they died out. Some have felt uncomfortable with Song of Songs because of its sexual implications. In the Old Testament, the intimacy of the marriage relationship is often used as an illustration of God and Israel. The whole book of Hosea is based around that theme. In the New Testament, the church is described as the bride of Christ. Revelation 19:7 says, "For the wedding of the Lamb has come, and his bride has made herself ready." Paul summed it up succinctly in Ephesians 5:31–32: "'For this reason a man will leave his father and mother and be united to his wife, and the two will become one flesh.' This is a profound mystery—but I am talking about Christ and the church."

Just in case there is some doubt about the meaning of "one flesh" being a sexual relationship, in 1 Corinthians 6:16, he spelled it out: "Do you not know that he who unites himself with a prostitute is one with her in body? For it is said, 'The two will become one flesh.'"

Adultery Is Sin. The next statement in Hebrews 13:4 that relates to sex is a negative statement: **God will judge the adulterer**. **Adulterer** is a specific Greek term, and the meaning is a married person who has a sexual relationship with another person to whom he or she is not married. This was one of the Ten Commandments: "You shall not commit adultery" (Deut. 5:18). The punishment was death (Deut. 22:22). Israel's relationship to God was often depicted under this illustration of the adulterous wife (see Hos. 4:14–18).

Sex Trade Is Perverse. The third element that deals with sex in Hebrews 13:4 is **all the sexually immoral**. The Greek term here is *pornos*. The word is related to sex, but the base meaning is "to sell." A whole family of terms relating to the selling of sex evolved out of this root word, including *pornography* (the selling of sex-related graphics). The KJV translates this word as "whoremongers." In other places it is translated as "fornicators," but the NIV's translation is all-inclusive. While **all the sexually immoral** might include prostitution, it also includes *pornography*, whether Internet or hard copy. *Pornos* would encompass sex clubs, books, magazines, videos, DVDs, movies, TV programs, and anything else where there is profit from the sale of sex.

WORDS FROM WESLEY

Hebrews 13:4

Marriage is honourable in—Or for all sorts of men, clergy as well as laity; though the Romanists teach otherwise; *and the bed undefiled*—Consistent with the highest purity; though many spiritual writers, so called, say it is only licensed whoredom; *but whoremongers and adulterers God will judge*—Though they frequently escape the sentence of men. (ENNT)

Freedom from Avarice (Heb. 13:5–6)

It is not necessary to possess money to be possessed by money. It is **the love of money** from which the writer enjoins readers to **keep your lives free from** (v. 5). First Timothy 6:10 is sometimes quoted out of context but emphasizes the same point: "For the love of money is a root of all kinds of evil. Some people, eager for money, have wandered from the faith and pierced themselves with many griefs."

The basic flaw with avarice, as the Hebrews writer saw it, is that it transfers a trust that belongs to God to material things. God's efficacy is in doubt when we have that type of infatuation with money. If contentment is not found without money as the primary ingredient, it will not be found with money as the main ingredient. Contentment is not a material physical entity and therefore cannot be bought.

Spiritual Authority (Heb. 13:7, 17–21)

There are three specific things to note in these passages about spiritual authority. The first is the element of tradition. The second is the spiritual leader's responsibility, and the third is the Christian's response to spiritual authority.

Tradition Is a Guide. **Remember your leaders, who spoke the word of God to you** (v. 7). John Wesley studied and often quoted from the early church fathers. If we forget where we came from, we will forget where we're going. North American culture puts so much emphasis on the isolated individual that it discounts history and community. The emphasis in this verse is not to idealize the past, but rather not to forget it. If you take note of the wounds of others, you can avoid the same wounds yourself. But beyond this, if you learn from the spiritual successes of others you can take thoughtful consideration **of their way of life and imitate their faith** (v. 7).

Leaders with Spiritual Authority Have Responsibility. There are specific things spiritual leaders do as outlined in Hebrews 13. They are to speak **the word of God** (v. 7). This indicates truth spoken with authority.

Next, their way of life must be as authentic as their manner of speaking. They don't preach one thing and live another. Their faith and life are inseparable, so others can imitate their faith. Spiritual leaders have a responsibility to speak with authority. Others under authority are to **obey your leaders** (v. 17). In Western society, we don't talk about this much. Culturally, we like to view ourselves as all being on a horizontal plane. But unless **submit to their authority** can be understood as something besides leaders taking authority and giving instructions, it must be assumed they are giving instructions that need obedient responses. There is a check to this authority: they **must give an account**. A part of what will come into account is motives (v. 18). So leaders with spiritual authority have a responsibility to use their authority overtly with the conscious understanding that they will one day give account to the perfect Judge who even knows motives.

WORDS FROM WESLEY

Hebrews 13:17

Obey them that have the rule over you—The word implies also, that lead or guide you: namely, in truth and holiness: *and submit yourselves*—Give up (not your conscience or judgment, but) your own will, in all things purely indifferent: *For they watch over your souls*—With all zeal and diligence, they guard and caution you against all danger, *as they that must give account*—To the great Shepherd for every part of their behaviour towards you. How vigilant then ought every pastor to be! How careful of every soul committed to his charge! *That they may do this*—Watch over you, *with joy, and not with groans*—He is not a good shepherd, who does not either rejoice over them, or groan for them. The groans of other creatures are heard: how much more shall these come up in the ears of God! Whoever answers this character of a Christian pastor, may undoubtedly demand this obedience. (ENNT)

Those Being Led Have Responsibility. There are five specific things that those under authority are to do: (1) Remember what spiritual leaders have said and done (v. 7); (2) imitate their lives (v. 7); (3) obey your leaders (v. 17); (4) submit to their authority (v. 17); and (5) pray for them (vv. 18–19).

Disceners of Truth (Heb. 13:8–16)

Do not be carried away by all kinds of strange teachings (v. 9). Before we can follow this instruction, we have to know truth. When truth is taught, strange teachings are easy to identify.

The next few verses (10–14) are a recap summary of the truth the writer has been teaching in the chapters that preceded chapter 13. The writer gave us some functional substitutes for some specific Old Testament teachings and rituals.

DISCUSSION

The Christian faith is not an inward faith only or even primarily. Christ transforms us from the inside out so that others can His reflection as we live out our faith in community.

1. Of all the exhortations found in Hebrews 13:1–10, which one do you think needs the greatest emphasis today? Why?

2. In what practical ways might a local church practice brotherly love?

3. If you wanted to promote hospitality among your Christian friends, what first steps would you take?

4. How might you "remember those in prison" (v. 3)?

5. What situations do you think pose the greatest danger to marital fidelity? To sexual purity?

6. How can a believer not be covetous in a materialistic world?

7. What elements of effective spiritual leadership do you see in verse 7?

8. What reasons to love Jesus do you find in verses 8–21?

PRAYER

Lord, keep us family-focused, hospitable, and ready to open our homes as You have need. Keep us focused on sound teaching, and help us imitate the faithful leaders You have provided.

WORDS FROM WESLEY WORKS CITED

ENNT: *Explanatory Notes upon the New Testament,* by John Wesley, M.A. Fourth American Edition. New York: J. Soule and T. Mason, for the Methodist Episcopal Church in the United States, 1818.

WJW: *The Works of John Wesley*. Third Edition, Complete and Unabridged. 14 vols. London: Wesleyan Methodist Book Room, 1872.

OTHER BOOKS IN THE
WESLEY BIBLE STUDIES SERIES

Genesis
Exodus
Leviticus through Deuteronomy
Joshua through Ruth
1 Samuel through 2 Chronicles
Ezra through Esther
Job through Song of Songs
Isaiah
Jeremiah through Daniel
Hosea through Malachi
Matthew
Mark
Luke
John
Acts
Romans
1–2 Corinthians
Galatians through Colossians and Philemon
1–2 Thessalonians
1 Timothy through Titus
Hebrews
James
1–2 Peter and Jude
1–3 John
Revelation